In the Kitchen with Grandma

Lydia E. Harris

HARVEST HOUSE PUBLISHERS
EUGENE, OREGON

Cover illustration and hand-lettering by Kristi Smith, Juicebox Designs

Author and family photos © by Jonathan M. Harris

Published in association with the literary agency of WordServe Literary Group, Ltd., www.wordserveliterary.com.

All oven temperatures are in degrees Fahrenheit.

In the Kitchen with Grandma
Copyright © 2019 by Lydia E. Harris
Published by Harvest House Publishers
Eugene, Oregon 97408
www.harvesthousepublishers.com

ISBN 978-0-7369-7587-2 (pbk.)
ISBN 978-0-7369-7588-9 (eBook)

Library of Congress Cataloging-in-Publication Data

Names: Harris, Lydia E., author.
Title: In the kitchen with grandma / Lydia E. Harris.
Description: Eugene, Oregon : Harvest House Publishers, [2019] | Includes index.
Identifiers: LCCN 2018049670 (print) | LCCN 2018053327 (ebook) | ISBN 9780736975889 (ebook) | ISBN 9780736975872 (pbk.)
Subjects: LCSH: Seasonal cooking. | Holiday cooking.
Classification: LCC TX714 (ebook) | LCC TX714 .H3656 2019 (print) | DDC 641.5/64--dc23
LC record available at https://lccn.loc.gov/2018049670

Printed in the United States of America

19 20 21 22 23 24 25 26 27 / VP-SK / 10 9 8 7 6 5 4 3 2 1

Dedicated with love to my five grandchildren,

Peter, Alex, Clara, Owen, and **Anna,**

who not only inspired me to write this cookbook
but also helped me create and test many of the recipes.

What a joy to spend time with you!

Also dedicated to my godly mother,

Helena Martens Siemens,

who cheerfully cooked for her large family of eight children.

"She provides food for her family…
and does not eat the bread of idleness."
PROVERBS 31:15,27

ACKNOWLEDGMENTS

I would like to thank everyone who helped
me and encouraged me in writing this cookbook.

Thank you to all who shared ideas and recipes,
tested and tasted recipes, edited my writing, and prayed for me.

A special thanks to my husband, Milt,
for his loving support and prayers.

Most of all, to God be the glory!

Contents

There is a time for everything, and a season for every activity under the heavens.

ECCLESIASTES 3:1

Tips for Stirring Up Tasty Memories Together

Taste and see that the LORD *is good.*

PSALM 34:8

"Grandma, you're a good cook," seven-year-old Anna said. I smiled. Then she added, "But when *I* cook with you, it tastes better!"

I heartily agree with Anna. When grandparents and grandkids cook together, the food tastes more delicious to everyone.

I've been cooking with my five grandkids since they were old enough to lick a spoon. How quickly the years pass. My oldest, Peter, is already a working young adult. I'm thankful I seized the moments to cook with him while I could. I savor precious kitchen memories with each of my grandkids.

I'm eager to share some of our recipes and ideas with you so you can stir up happy times too. Whether your grandkids live nearby or only visit occasionally, with this cookbook you can make memories together. Feel free to add comments and ideas in the margins to make this a treasured keepsake of your experiences.

Here are some tips to make cooking together a wonderful time.

Spoonfuls of Difficulty

The recipes are rated with 1, 2, or 3 spoonfuls of difficulty, with 1 being the easiest to make. The 2 spoonful recipes are moderate in difficulty, and the 3 spoonful recipes are more challenging and take longer to prepare.

But even the most difficult recipes include simple things a young child can do to help. Also, Grandma can preprep some of the recipes.

Prep Time

The time listed is an estimate so you can decide if you have enough time for the recipe. But once you begin, relax and take your time. The longer it takes, the more memories you make.

Gluten-Free

Numerous recipes are listed with gluten-free options. However, it is important to carefully check your ingredients to ensure each one is gluten-free. Brands vary.

Safety First

Grandchildren of all ages will use this cookbook, and their abilities and cooking skills will vary. With Grandma beside them, they will have the help and supervision they need. Take extra care when using sharp knives, electrical appliances, and hot stoves.

Cleanup

Cooking and eating are fun, but cleaning up is not anyone's favorite part. I fill the sink with warm, soapy water and add dirty cooking utensils to soak while we cook. This makes cleanup easier.

A Spoonful of Sharing

When I first considered writing this cookbook years ago, this verse motivated me: "Remember your Creator in the days of your youth" (Ecclesiastes 12:1). I wanted to encourage grandparents to teach their grandchildren about God at a young age.

Cooking and eating together provide time to chat. For some recipes I've included discussion prompts. In the Bible, Moses writes about God's commands and says to share them during everyday living. "These commandments that I give you today are to be on your hearts. Impress them on your children. Talk about them when you sit at home and when you walk along the road, when you lie down and when you get up" (Deuteronomy 6:6-7).

When it seems natural and appropriate, I encourage you to be intentional about sharing your faith and godly values with your grandchildren—especially when you cook together.

Emphasize Relationships, Not Recipes

Cooking together is about *relationships*, not recipes. We don't need to create blue-ribbon-winning foods or ones to be featured in a magazine. It's about our presence, not perfection. It's more about the process than the product.

This cookbook is full of fun and good eating. It's also filled with love and prayers. I hope you enjoy making these grandma-approved, grandkid-tested recipes. Grandfathers, parents, caregivers, and teachers could also use this cookbook to cook with kids.

Celebrate the Holidays

In the Kitchen with Grandma is designed to use any day or season of the year. But near the end you'll find menus and themes for holidays and special days. I hope those creative ideas will inspire you to celebrate together all year—as often as you can.

I wish you oodles of spoon-lickin' good times in the kitchen with your grandkids. And when you cook together, the food will taste better than ever!

Happy cooking!

Grandma Tea
(as my grandkids call me)

Spring

Kites flying, daffodils blooming, and chicks hatching. A time of new life and new beginnings. Spring into the fun of the season and celebrate these special holidays together: St. Patrick's Day, Easter, Cinco de Mayo, and Mother's Day.

The flowers appear on the earth, the time of singing has come,
and the voice of the turtledove is heard in our land.
SONG OF SOLOMON 2:12 NKJV

Spring

Notes:

Butterfly Waffles

These colorful, tasty butterflies are ready to flutter right into your mouth! (This recipe is for one serving, but you can increase the ingredients to fit the servings needed.)

Difficulty: 

Prep time: 15 minutes
Gluten-free option: Use gluten-free waffles and sausages

Gather with Grandma

1 square or round waffle
(homemade or ready-made frozen)
1 cooked sausage link
Fresh fruit to make colorful spots on wings
(kiwi, strawberries, and blueberries)
1 red apple
Powdered sugar
Syrup or honey (to serve with the waffle)
Whipped cream or yogurt

See page 38 for Homemade Whipped Cream.

Make with Grandma

1. Toast a waffle. Put it on a plate and cut it in half to make two wings. For a square waffle, cut it in half diagonally and place the points together. For a round waffle, cut it in half and place the rounded sides together.
2. Add a cooked sausage for the body between the waffle wings. Warm the butterfly in the microwave.
3. Decorate the butterfly with blueberries and slices of kiwi and strawberries.
4. Add two thin strips of a red apple for the antennae.
5. Dust with powdered sugar.
6. Serve the waffle with syrup or honey, whipped cream or yogurt, and more fresh fruit.

Makes 1 serving

Notes:

SPRING

Crock-Pot Irish Stew

A hearty main dish made with root vegetables, which are plentiful in Ireland. *(From the kitchen of Grandma Kathleen in Ireland, who has 20 grandchildren.)*

Difficulty: 

Prep time: 35 minutes
Cooking time: 5 or more hours
Gluten-free

Gather with Grandma

1 lb. beef stew meat, cut into 1-inch cubes
1 T. oil
1 medium-sized onion, cut into eighths
2 or 3 beef bouillon cubes
2 cups warm water
3 cups potatoes, peeled and cut into large chunks
2 cups carrots, peeled and cut into thick slices
½ cup turnips, cut into 1-inch chunks (optional)
2 T. cornstarch (optional)

Make with Grandma

1. Brown the meat in the oil on medium high.
2. Place the meat, onion, and browned drippings into the Crock-Pot. Dissolve the bouillon cubes in the water and add them to the pot. Cover.
3. Cook on high for three hours or until the meat is tender.
4. Add potatoes, carrots, and turnips. If needed, add more water to cover the vegetables. Cook on high for two more hours or until the vegetables are tender.
5. The stew should be thick, not runny like soup. If the stew is thin, mix 2 tablespoons cornstarch with ¼ cup cold water and add it to the stew. Simmer the stew until it thickens.
6. Add salt and pepper to taste.

Serves 6 to 8

Shortcut: Instead of fresh vegetables, use two (16 oz.) packages frozen stew vegetables.

Notes:

Easter Egg-Stravaganza

For this fun-filled lunch, purchase plastic eggs to fill with bite-sized finger foods that are eggs-actly what your grandkids like. Use baskets or empty egg cartons as lunch boxes. My preschool-age granddaughter requested this lunch year-round. Now in grade school, she still enjoys selecting the foods, filling the eggs, hunting for them, and then wondering which egg holds which food.

Difficulty: 

Prep time: 20 minutes
Gluten-free option: Select gluten-free foods to fill the eggs

Gather with Grandma

1 empty egg carton or basket per person
12 clean plastic eggs for each person
Bite-sized foods to fill the eggs, such as:
- Mini sandwiches
- Cubes of cheese
- Strips of ham
- Goldfish crackers
- Popcorn
- Carrot circles
- Olives
- Sliced pickles or cucumbers
- Grapes
- Blueberries
- Cherries
- Craisins
- Mini muffins
- Small candies, such as jelly beans, chocolate eggs, or M&M's

Make with Grandma

1. Select foods you like from the list or add your own. Include a variety of foods from different food groups (fruits, vegetables, bread, protein, and sweets).
2. Prepare the foods and place them in small bowls on the table.

Notes:

SPRING

3. Each person fills 12 plastic eggs with his or her favorite foods. If necessary, wrap the foods in plastic wrap. Then place the eggs in a basket or carton.
4. Refrigerate the eggs until you are ready for the egg hunt.
5. For an Easter egg hunt with more than one person, place stickers on the eggs to identify who they belong to, or use a different color of plastic eggs for each person.
6. Each person hides someone else's eggs indoors.
7. Hunt for your own eggs and place them in an egg carton or basket. Then choose a cozy place to share lunch.
8. Open each egg, place the food on a plate, and nibble away. If you're still hungry, refill the eggs or choose from the leftovers in the bowls.

Makes 12 eggs per person

A Spoonful of Sharing

To help tell the resurrection story, leave one egg empty to represent Jesus's empty tomb. Or write out this verse and enclose it in the empty egg: "He is not here; he has risen" (Matthew 28:6). What do you like about Easter? Share special Easter memories with each other.

Notes:

SPRING

Ham and Swiss Cheese Melts

These delicious sandwiches are a great way to use leftover Easter ham. To our family, they taste like a feast! *(A favorite from the kitchen of Mimi Audrey.)*

Difficulty:

Prep time: 20 minutes
Baking time: 20 minutes
Gluten-free option: Use gluten-free bread or rolls and Worcestershire sauce

Gather with Grandma

12 Hawaiian sweet rolls (small dinner-size rolls)
6 slices Swiss cheese
½ lb. ham, thinly sliced
⅓ cup (½ stick plus 1 T.) butter, melted
¾ tsp. Worcestershire sauce
¾ tsp. Dijon mustard
1 tsp. minced dried onion

Make with Grandma

1. Preheat the oven to 350°.
2. Slice the rolls in half horizontally.
3. Cut each slice of cheese into 4 squares and put 2 squares into each roll.
4. Fold slices of ham into layers and place 1 folded slice inside each roll.
5. Place the buns in an ungreased 9 x 13-inch baking pan.
6. In a saucepan, combine and heat the butter, Worcestershire sauce, and mustard. Stir until well blended. Add the dried onion. Spoon some of the mixture over each bun.
7. Bake for 15 to 20 minutes or until the rolls are browned and the cheese is melted. Remove the pan of rolls from the oven and place it on a cooling rack. Enjoy these melts while they are still warm. Refrigerate the leftovers. They also taste delicious cold or reheated.

Makes 6 servings with two buns per person

Notes:

SPRING

Sealed with a Quiche

When I asked some moms and grandmas what they would like for brunch on Mother's Day, they said, "Quiche." Using a ready-made crust makes this recipe simple to prepare. While the quiche bakes, you can also make Sweet or Savory Bacon Knots (see page 26) to go with it.

Difficulty: 

Prep time: 25 minutes
Baking time: 35 to 40 minutes
Gluten-free option: Use a gluten-free crust or bake the quiche without a crust

Gather with Grandma

1 unbaked 9-inch piecrust (ready-made or homemade)
¾ cup chopped ham (chopped thin slices from the deli or a thicker ham steak cut into small cubes)
1½ cups cheddar cheese, grated
½ cup Swiss cheese, grated (or your favorite cheese)
4 eggs, beaten
1½ cups milk (2% or whole)
1 tsp. dried onion flakes (optional)
Dash of pepper
Parsley and cherry tomatoes for garnish (optional)

See page 156 for the piecrust recipe I use with Cascade Blackberry Pie.

Make with Grandma

1. Preheat the oven to 375°.
2. Place 1 piecrust in the bottom of a 9-inch pie pan.
3. Distribute the ham and cheeses evenly in the pie shell.
4. Mix together the eggs, milk, onion, and pepper. Pour the mixture into the crust.
5. Bake the quiche for 35 to 40 minutes until the egg mixture is no longer runny. Test by inserting a table knife near the center to see if it comes out clean. Cool for 10 minutes or until the egg mixture is firm.

Notes:

SPRING

6. Garnish the quiche with cherry tomatoes and parsley. Cut into pie-shaped wedges. Refrigerate leftovers.

Serves 6

Variations: *Crustless Quiche:* Spray a 9-inch pie pan with nonstick cooking spray. Mix all the ingredients together. Pour the quiche mixture into the pan and bake.

Vegetarian version: Omit the ham and add ½ cup sliced, cooked mushrooms and 1 cup chopped steamed vegetables of your choice, such as spinach, broccoli, or any combination you like. Diced red, orange, and green peppers add a colorful confetti look. Be sure to drain the vegetables well before adding to avoid a watery quiche.

A Spoonful of Sharing

What makes your mother special? In the Bible, we are told to honor our father and mother, and God will bless us if we do. (See Ephesians 6:1-2 and Exodus 20:12.) How can you show love to your parents and honor them?

Notes:

SPRING

Sombrero Skillet Pie

Simmer this up as a hearty main dish or appetizer. The chips around the edge look like the brim of a hat.

Difficulty:

Prep time: 30 minutes
Gluten-free option: Use gluten-free corn tortilla chips

Gather with Grandma

1 lb. lean ground beef
1 cup frozen corn
1 (8 oz.) can tomato sauce
1 (14.5 oz.) can diced tomatoes
1 T. minced dried onion
1 tsp. sugar
½ tsp. salt
½ tsp. chili powder (more if you like it spicier)
1 cup cheddar cheese, grated
Corn tortilla chips
Black olives and avocado (optional)

Make with Grandma

1. Fry the ground beef in a skillet over medium heat until the beef is browned. Drain the grease.
2. Stir in the corn, tomato sauce, tomatoes, onion, sugar, salt, and chili powder.
3. Turn the heat to low and simmer the mixture uncovered for 20 minutes, stirring occasionally. Then sprinkle the cheese on top to melt.
4. Before serving, arrange chips in a ring around the inside edge of the skillet. Top with sliced black olives and avocado if desired.
5. Serve directly from the skillet and pass a basket of extra tortilla chips.

Serves 6 for a main dish or about 12 for an appetizer

Notes:

SPRING

Creamy Fruit Salad Dressing and Dip

Pineapple juice gives this creamy dressing a luscious flavor. *(A favorite recipe from the kitchen of Great-Grandma Erna, my sister.)*

Difficulty:

Prep time: 15 minutes
Chilling time: 30 minutes or longer
Gluten-free

Gather with Grandma

¼ cup (½ stick) butter, melted
½ cup granulated sugar
⅓ cup pineapple juice
2 eggs, well beaten
½ cup sour cream

Make with Grandma

1. In a saucepan, combine the butter, sugar, pineapple juice, and eggs. Cook the sauce on medium heat until thickened, stirring constantly.
2. Chill the mixture in the refrigerator for 30 minutes or until completely cooled.
3. Stir the sour cream into the cooled dressing.
4. Refrigerate the dressing until ready to serve. It tastes best if well chilled.
5. Serve it as a dressing or dip with fresh fruit or fruit salad. It also tastes delicious drizzled over cake, cobbler, and scones.
6. Refrigerate the leftovers. It keeps in the refrigerator for about 1 week.

Makes 1¼ cups

Tip: Buy individual 6 oz. cans of pineapple juice or save the juice from canned pineapple.

Notes:

SPRING

Fancy Fruit Bouquets

Make a beautiful, edible fresh fruit bouquet for Mom or someone special.

Difficulty:

Prep time: 20 to 30 minutes
Gluten-free

Gather with Grandma

Short drinking glass to use as a vase
Parsley, washed, to use as greens for the bouquet
Leafy celery stalks from inside the bunch, for bouquet greens (optional)
Wooden skewers or picks, 6 inches long
Fruits of your choice, such as:
- Fresh strawberries with stems, washed
- Melons, cut into cubes or balls
- Red and green grapes, washed
- Other favorite seasonal fruits

Make with Grandma

1. Fill the drinking glass half full of water. Place a small bunch of parsley into the glass. The parsley height should be about 3 inches above the top of the glass. If desired, also add leafy celery stalks for greenery.
2. Poke each strawberry onto a skewer with the pointed ends of the berries up to look like rosebuds.
3. Arrange the "rosebuds" in the glass at varying heights to make a bouquet. The posies can stick up above the parsley or nestle in the greens.
4. Place other fruits on picks and add them to the bouquet. For example, alternate red and green grapes on one pick and melon balls on another. If you wish, cut some fruits with small cookie cutters and add them on picks. A small circle of cantaloupe with a grape in the center makes a colorful flower. You can be as creative as you like.
5. If serving a larger group of people, make several bouquets or individual ones for each person.

6. Serve the bouquets plain or with a small bowl of Creamy Fruit Salad Dressing and Dip (see page 19).

Make as many as needed

A Spoonful of Sharing

What is your favorite kind of fruit? Just as the fruits in your bouquet vary, people are different too. What is one thing you especially like about yourself? The Bible says we are "fearfully and wonderfully made" (Psalm 139:14). God made each of us special, and together we make a beautiful bouquet.

Notes:

Notes:

SPRING

Irish Fresh Fruit Flag

Create a delicious Irish flag that's both colorful and healthy. It's easy to do with green, white, and orange fruits.

Difficulty:

Prep time: 15 minutes
Gluten-free

Gather with Grandma

Green fruits: grapes, kiwi, green apples, and/or honeydew melon
White fruits: bananas, peeled pears, and/or apples
Orange fruits: oranges, peaches, nectarines, apricots, and/or cantaloupe

Make with Grandma

1. Wash the fruit. Peel it if needed.
2. Cut the fruit into small chunks or slices.
3. On a large rectangular platter or pan, arrange the fruits to look like the Irish flag. Green fruits go in a vertical row on the left, white fruits down the center, and orange fruits on the right. You can use one kind of fruit for each color or a variety.
4. Serve with Creamy Fruit Salad Dressing and Dip (see page 19).

Serves 6 or more

A Spoonful of Sharing

St. Patrick's Day is celebrated on March 17. This holiday began as a holy day to honor St. Patrick, a Christian missionary to Ireland. Patrick was 16 years old when he was kidnapped into slavery in Ireland. Years later, Patrick became a Christian, escaped from slavery, and then returned to preach salvation to the Irish. What can we learn from St. Patrick's life?

Notes:

Mexican Veggie Flag

Create an edible Mexican symbol with vegetables that are the same colors as the Mexican flag: green, white, and red. My seven-year-old granddaughter enjoyed choosing the veggies she knew her family liked and arranging them to make this crunchy flag.

Difficulty: 

Prep time: 15 minutes
Gluten-free

Gather with Grandma

Green vegetables, such as fresh broccoli, snap peas, celery, zucchini, and cucumber

White vegetables, such as cauliflower and jicama ("HEE-kah-mah," also known as a Mexican potato)

Red vegetables, such as cherry tomatoes, radishes, and red peppers

Dip, such as salsa, sour cream, guacamole, or ranch

See recipe for Ranch Dressing and Dip on page 148.

Make with Grandma

1. Wash the vegetables. Peel the jicama before serving.
2. Cut the vegetables into small chunks, slices, or strips (2 to 3 bites per piece).
3. On about an 8 x 10-inch rectangular platter, tray, or cake pan, arrange the veggies to look like the Mexican flag. Place green vegetables in a vertical row on the left, white vegetables down the center, and red vegetables on the right side.
4. Serve the veggie flag with your favorite red, white, or green dips in small bowls on the side.

Serves 8 or more

Notes:

SPRING

Peter Rabbit's Carrot Patch and Hummus

Peter Rabbit isn't the only one who would enjoy munching on these tasty vegetables and hummus dip.

Difficulty:

Prep time: 15 minutes
Gluten-free

Gather with Grandma

1 (10 oz.) container hummus
Small peeled carrots (3 or more carrots per person)
Fresh parsley
Additional fresh veggies of your choice (optional)

Make with Grandma

1. Place the hummus in a small flat bowl. This is the "soil" for the garden.
2. Using a toothpick, poke a hole in the larger end of each carrot.
3. Place a small sprig of parsley into the carrot holes.
4. Plant the carrots in the hummus soil.
5. If desired, set the hummus with planted carrots on a larger plate. Add additional fresh veggies of your choice around the hummus bowl.

6 to 8 servings

Tip: For individual carrot patches, use small, ¼-pint jars or short clear plastic cups. Add hummus and carrots to the individual containers. The mini gardens look cute by each place setting. You could also plant radishes in the hummus if you wish.

A Spoonful of Sharing

Peter Rabbit says, "Casting all your care upon him; for he [carrot] careth for you" (1 Peter 5:7 KJV). How have you seen God care for you?

Notes:

Sparkling Sonrise Fruit Parfaits

The pineapple ring peeking over the horizon reminds us of the wonderful sunrise surprise on Easter—Jesus's resurrection! *(Recipe inspired by my sister Helen's cooking.)*

Difficulty:

Prep time: 15 minutes
Gluten-free

Gather with Grandma

Clear goblets or juice glasses
Pineapple chunks, fresh or canned
Cantaloupe balls or chunks
Green grapes, washed
Pineapple rings, cut in half
Sparkling cider, chilled

Make with Grandma

1. Layer the fruit in individual glasses in this order, starting from the bottom: pineapple chunks, cantaloupe, and grapes.
2. To represent the sun rising, tuck the half pineapple rings inside the glasses, standing up on the inside of each parfait. Chill the parfaits until you're ready to serve them.
3. Just before serving, pour cider over the chilled fruit.

Make as many individual servings as you need

Variation: Use a combination of any three colors of fruits that would taste good with sparkling cider.

Notes:

SPRING

Sweet or Savory Bacon Knots

These are crisp and tasty. Make your bacon sweet with brown sugar or savory with herbs from your cupboard.

Difficulty:

Prep time: 15 minutes
Baking time: 20 to 30 minutes
Gluten-free option: Select gluten-free bacon

Gather with Grandma

Bacon slices
Brown sugar
Maple syrup
Seasonings of your choice

Make with Grandma

1. Preheat the oven to 350°. Line a 9 x 13-inch pan with aluminum foil. Or prepare a shallow pan with a rack so the grease can drip off while cooking.
2. If the bacon has more fat on the end than you like, trim off excess fat. Rinse the bacon in water so the sugar and spices stick better.
3. Fold each bacon slice in half, tie it into a loose knot, and place it in the pan. Make as many as needed.
4. For sweet knots, sprinkle the bacon with brown sugar or drizzle it with maple syrup. For savory knots, lightly sprinkle the bacon with seasonings, such as Italian or black pepper. You can also make them sweet and savory by adding sugar as well as spices to the knots. Have fun experimenting with combinations of herbs and spices that sound good to you.
5. Bake the knots for 15 minutes and then check them for doneness. Continue baking as needed until the strips are as crisp as you like. Cooking time will also depend on the thickness of the bacon.
6. Remove the pan from the oven and set it on a cooling rack. Place the bacon knots on a plate with a paper towel to absorb the excess grease.
7. Serve hot. Refrigerate leftovers.

Make as many as you wish, at least 2 per person

Notes:

SPRING

Apple Posies and Buzzy Bee Snacks

These treats are almost too cute to eat, but they are fun to create and share.

Difficulty:

Prep time: 30 minutes
Gluten-free: Apple Posies only (if served with gluten-free dip)

Gather with Grandma

Apple Posy (makes two posies)

1 green apple, such as Granny Smith
1 red apple
Caramel dip or caramel sauce

Buzzy Bees

½ cup vanilla wafer crumbs, crushed very fine
½ cup powdered sugar
¼ cup plus 2 T. creamy peanut butter
1 tsp. cinnamon, for stripes
¼ cup sliced almonds, for wings
Mini chocolate chips, for eyes
Pretzel snaps for honeycomb (square pretzels with holes in them) (optional)
Honey (optional)

Make with Grandma

1. In the center of a 6-inch or larger plate, spread a thin layer of caramel dip or sauce.
2. Core the apples and then cut one-half a red apple and one-half a green apple into slices for each posy.
3. Alternate the red and green apple slices on the caramel so they touch in the center and make a flower with apple petals. Repeat to make another posy on a separate plate.
4. To make the bees, combine the wafer crumbs and sugar. Mix in the peanut butter with your hands.

Notes:

SPRING

5. Shape the mixture into oval bite-sized bees, using a heaping teaspoon of the mixture for each bee.
6. To make stripes across the body of the bee, dip a toothpick into water and then roll it in cinnamon. Press the cinnamon toothpick across the top of the bee to make 3 stripes. Dip the toothpick in water and cinnamon as needed.
7. Add an almond slice on each side of the bee's body for wings. On the front of the bee, poke in chocolate chips for eyes.
8. Place a bee in the center of each apple flower. Add more bees around the edges of the posies. If desired, drizzle pretzel snaps with honey and place them by the bees for honeycombs.

Makes 2 apple posies and 12 to 16 buzzy bees

Variations: Replace the caramel on the plate with peanut butter, honey, or cream cheese.

A Spoonful of Sharing

While you eat the apple slices, think about Psalm 17:8: "Keep me as the apple of your eye; hide me in the shadow of your wings." *Apple* in this verse refers to the pupil of the eye. Just as we carefully protect this "seeing center," God cherishes us and protects us too.

Notes:

Bananapillars

When my grade-school-aged grandson, Alex, made this snack, he drew a picture of the bananapillar before eating it. After he ate the apple slices from the bananapillar, he replaced them with more slices for seconds.

Difficulty:

Prep time: 15 minutes
Gluten-free option: Use gluten-free pretzels

Gather with Grandma (for each bananapillar)

1 lettuce leaf
1 medium-sized banana
1 red apple or red pear
2 raisins
6 pretzel sticks
2 T. shredded coconut or finely grated cheddar cheese (optional)

Make with Grandma

1. Wash the lettuce leaf, pat it dry, and place it on a plate.
2. Peel a banana and place it on the lettuce leaf.
3. Cut a ¼-inch deep V-shaped slice out of the banana 1 inch from the end of the banana.
4. Make 5 more V-shaped slices 1 inch apart.
5. Cut a small red apple into quarters and remove the core.
6. Cut 1 apple quarter into 5 to 6 thin slices.
7. Place 1 apple slice, peel side up, into each V-shaped cut in the banana.
8. For the caterpillar's eyes, gently press two raisins into one end of the banana.
9. For the legs, break pretzel sticks in half and place six pieces on each side, pressing them into the banana.
10. For a fuzzy caterpillar, sprinkle the banana with coconut or grated cheese.

Make as many as you wish

Notes:

SPRING

Cinnamon Chips

Crisp and tasty! Grandkids love these, and so do grandparents. "Grandpa was all over these," said Grandma Elaine.

Difficulty:

Prep time: 10 minutes
Baking time: 10 minutes

Gather with Grandma

4 6-inch flour tortillas
¼ cup granulated sugar
1 tsp. cinnamon
Butter-flavored nonstick cooking spray

Make with Grandma

1. Preheat the oven to 350°. Prepare a baking sheet with nonstick cooking spray.
2. Stir together the sugar and cinnamon. Pour the mixture onto a dinner plate.
3. Spray both sides of a tortilla with nonstick cooking spray.
4. Dip both sides of the tortilla into the sugar mixture.
5. Cut the tortilla in half with a pizza cutter or knife, then cut each half into 4 pie-shaped chips.
6. Place the chips in a single layer on a large cookie sheet. Repeat with each tortilla.
7. Bake the chips for 8 to 10 minutes, until lightly browned and crisp.
8. Carefully remove the pan with chips from the oven and cool them. Serve the chips with Fiesta Fruit Salsa (see page 31).

Serves 3 to 4

Fiesta Fruit Salsa

Sweet, juicy, and refreshing.

Difficulty:

Prep time: 30 minutes
Gluten-free

Gather with Grandma

2 kiwis
1 lb. fresh strawberries (about 1½ cups)
1 Golden Delicious apple
½ cup canned pineapple tidbits or crushed pineapple
¼ cup strawberry or raspberry jam

Make with Grandma

1. Peel and dice the kiwis.
2. Wash the strawberries, remove the stems, and dice the berries.
3. Wash, core, and dice the apple.
4. Drain the pineapple, and use only the fruit.
5. In a large bowl, combine all the fruits.
6. Add jam to the fruit and mix well.
7. Cover and chill the mixture in the refrigerator for at least 15 minutes.
8. Serve the salsa with Cinnamon Chips (see page 30) or as a topping for pudding or ice cream.

Makes 3½ to 4 cups fruit salsa

Notes:

Notes:

SPRING

Ladybug Cheese and Crackers

This cute, easy-to-make ladybug adds a lot of color to a plate with cheese and crackers. Eat the ladybug before it flies away.

Difficulty:

Prep time: 15 minutes
Gluten-free option: Serve with gluten-free crackers

Gather with Grandma (for each ladybug)

1 mini Babybel cheese, cellophane wrapper removed
2 or 3 black olives
Spinach or lettuce leaf, washed
Shoestring potato sticks (optional)
Crackers of your choice

Make with Grandma

1. Pull the tab to begin opening the cheese. Leave the red wax wrapper together at the top. Spread it slightly apart at the bottom to make ladybug wings.
2. With a toothpick, attach a black olive to the front of the cheese for a head.
3. Cut another olive into small pieces to use as spots on the ladybug's wings. To make round spots, cut an olive in half lengthwise and use a plastic straw to poke out olive circles. (It's easier to cut the circles from the inside of the olive.)
4. Place the ladybug on a green leaf. Add the olive spots. If desired, add 3 short potato sticks on each side for legs.
5. Serve the ladybug with your favorite crackers.

Make as many as needed

Fun fact: Not all ladybugs are girls!

Notes:

SPRING

7UP Shamrock Biscuits

The 7UP in these buttery, melt-in-your-mouth biscuits makes them rise before your eyes. You'll want to eat them all year long, but for St. Patrick's Day tint the dough green and cut it into shamrocks.

Difficulty:

Prep time: 20 minutes
Baking time: 10 minutes
Gluten-free option: Use gluten-free baking mix

Gather with Grandma

¼ cup (½ stick) butter, melted
2½ cups baking mix, divided (e.g., Bisquick)
½ cup sour cream
½ cup 7UP
Green sprinkles (optional)

Make with Grandma

1. Preheat the oven to 450°.
2. Pour the melted butter into a baking pan with sides.
3. In a large bowl, mix together 2¼ cups baking mix and the sour cream.
4. Add the 7UP and mix the dough by hand. It will be sticky.
5. Sprinkle a clean surface with ¼ cup baking mix. Lightly knead the biscuit dough, mixing in the baking mix. If the dough is still too sticky, add 1 or 2 more tablespoons of the baking mix at a time.
6. Roll the dough 1 inch thick. Cut out the biscuits with a shamrock cookie cutter. (If you don't have one, see the note below.)
7. To make green shamrocks, sprinkle the biscuits with green sugar before baking them.
8. Place the biscuits in the pan with the melted butter.
9. Bake the biscuits for 10 minutes or until golden brown. Watch closely so they don't burn. Lower the oven temperature to 400° if necessary.
10. When the biscuits are baked, place the pan on a cooling rack. Serve the biscuits with butter, jam, or for more green—mint jelly.

Notes:

SPRING

Makes 10 to 12 2-inch biscuits

Tip: To make shamrock-shaped biscuits, cut the biscuits with a small heart-shaped cutter. When you put the points of three hearts together, it looks like the three leaves of a shamrock. Bake as directed.

To make green shamrocks, add 1 or 2 drops green food coloring to the dough before kneading it and rolling it out to cut.

A Spoonful of Sharing

What a surprise—7UP in biscuits! As you make and eat the biscuits, talk about whether God is ever surprised. The Bible says God knows everything before it even happens. "Before a word is on my tongue you, Lord, know it completely" (Psalm 139:4). Although God is not surprised, sometimes He does surprising things. What has God done that surprised you?

Notes:

Hot Cross Buns

Start with frozen rolls, add fruit and spices, and create a yummy aroma in your kitchen. Add crosses with frosting to celebrate Easter.

Difficulty:

Prep time: 25 minutes
Rising time: 1 hour or longer
Baking time: 15 to 20 minutes

Gather with Grandma

Rolls

18 frozen yeast rolls
⅓ cup golden raisins
⅓ cup brown sugar
1 tsp. cardamom
1 tsp. cinnamon
1 egg
1 T. water

Frosting

½ cup powdered sugar
1 T. softened butter
1 tsp. milk
¼ tsp. vanilla

Make with Grandma

1. Thaw the rolls according to the package directions until you can cut through the dough, but the rolls are still cold.
2. While the dough thaws, mix together the raisins, brown sugar, and spices.
3. Grease or spray a 9 x 13-inch pan with nonstick cooking spray.
4. To make each hot cross bun, combine one and one-half rolls. On a lightly floured surface, press the rolls together and flatten the dough to a 3-inch circle. Add about 1 tablespoon of the filling mixture and press it into the flattened dough.
5. Roll up each bun like a jelly roll, and then shape it into a round ball by

Notes:

SPRING

tucking the ends underneath. Place the rolls into the baking pan with the seam on the bottom and the rounded side up.

6. Shape all the rolls, and place them in the pan, leaving spaces between them to rise.
7. Cover the rolls and set them in a warm place to rise for 1 hour or until they fill the pan.
8. Preheat the oven to 350°.
9. Before baking, beat the egg with a fork, add 1 tablespoon water, and brush the buns with the egg glaze.
10. Bake the buns according to the package directions, about 15 minutes or until the buns are brown. Remove the pan of rolls from the oven and place it on a cooling rack. After 5 minutes, remove the rolls from the baking pan to a cooling rack.
11. While the rolls cool, mix together the frosting ingredients. If the frosting is too thin, add more powdered sugar. If too stiff, add a few more drops of milk.
12. When the rolls are completely cool, add the crosses. To make crosses on the buns, snip off a small corner of a plastic sandwich bag. Add the frosting in the snipped corner and seal the bag. Squeeze the frosting through the hole to make a cross design on each roll.

Makes 12 buns

Shortcut: Use ready-made frosting for the crosses.

A Spoonful of Sharing

As you add the crosses to the buns, talk about Jesus's death and resurrection. To learn more, read the story of Jesus's resurrection in one of the Gospels: Matthew 28, Mark 16, Luke 24, or John 20.

Apple Enchiladas

Try this simple south-of-the-border version of apple pie.

Difficulty:

Prep time: 20 minutes
Baking time: 20 to 25 minutes
Gluten-free option: Use gluten-free tortillas

Gather with Grandma

1 (21 oz.) can apple pie filling
1 tsp. ground cinnamon
8 6-inch flour tortillas
½ cup water
⅓ cup granulated sugar
⅓ cup brown sugar, firmly packed
2 T. butter
½ tsp. vanilla
Vanilla ice cream (optional)

Make with Grandma

1. Preheat the oven to 350°. Spray the bottom of a 9 x 13-inch baking pan with nonstick cooking spray.
2. In a medium-sized bowl, mix together the apple pie filling and cinnamon.
3. Spoon ¼ cup apple filling evenly down the center of a tortilla. Roll it up and place the enchilada in the baking pan with the flap down, so it won't unroll. Repeat with the other tortillas.
4. In a medium-sized saucepan, combine the water, sugars, and butter. Cook over medium heat, stirring constantly with a wooden spoon. When the sauce comes to a boil, reduce the heat, and simmer it for 3 minutes, stirring occasionally. Remove the saucepan from the heat and stir in the vanilla.
5. Spoon the sauce evenly over the enchiladas.
6. Bake for 20 to 25 minutes or until golden brown. Remove from the oven.
7. Allow the enchiladas to cool slightly. Serve warm with ice cream if desired.

Makes 8 enchiladas

Notes:

SPRING

Notes:

SPRING

Homemade Whipped Cream

My grandkids would eat this by the spoonful or bowlful if I let them! Of course, they also like to lick the whipped cream left on the beaters.

Difficulty: 

Prep time: 10 minutes
Gluten-free

Gather with Grandma

1 cup heavy whipping cream
1 T. granulated sugar
1 T. powdered sugar
½ tsp. vanilla

Make with Grandma

1. With an electric mixer, whip the cream on high speed until stiff peaks form.
2. Stir in sugars and vanilla. Refrigerate leftovers.

Makes 2 cups

Note: My grandson Owen and I discovered a way to keep the whipping cream from splattering. Cover the mixing bowl with a piece of wax paper slightly larger than the bowl. Cut a slit to the center of the wax paper and cut a hole in the center that the beaters fit through. When you beat the cream, the covering keeps the whipping cream from splattering out.

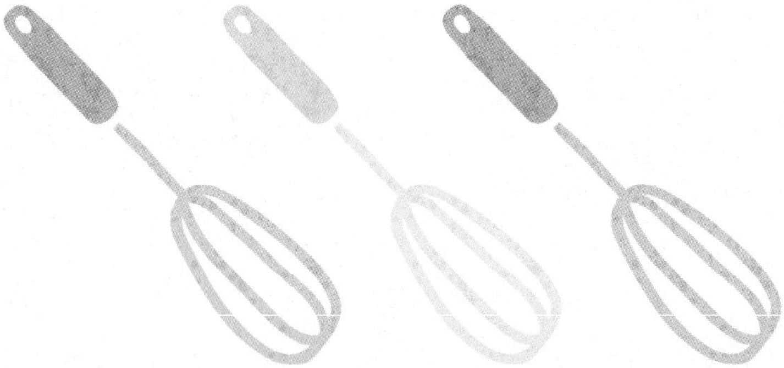

Notes:

SPRING

Hugs and Kisses for Mom

Easy and fun to make. Bite into a flaky biscuit to find a warm, melted chocolate surprise. *(A favorite recipe from Kellie's kitchen.)*

Difficulty:

Prep time: 10 minutes
Baking time: 15 minutes

Gather with Grandma

20 Hershey's Kisses, unwrapped
(or use some Hugs and some Kisses)
1 (7.5 oz.) tube refrigerated biscuits, regular size
3 T. melted butter
Cinnamon to sprinkle on top before baking
Powdered sugar to sprinkle on top after baking

Make with Grandma

1. Preheat the oven to 350°. Spray an 8-inch round cake pan with nonstick cooking spray.
2. Cut each biscuit in half.
3. Flatten the biscuit dough and put 1 Kiss in the center. Wrap the dough around it, making sure the dough is sealed around the chocolate.
4. Arrange the balls in a circle around the edge of the prepared pan. Or arrange them in the shape of a heart.
5. Drizzle melted butter over the biscuits and sprinkle them lightly with cinnamon.
6. Bake for 15 minutes or until the biscuits are golden brown.
7. Remove the biscuits from the oven. Cool them for a few minutes. Then carefully turn the pan upside down onto a serving plate. Sprinkle the biscuits with powdered sugar. Serve them warm while the chocolate is soft. If you serve these to Mom, be sure to give her a real hug and a kiss as well.

Makes 20 small chocolate-filled biscuits

Tip: To make a coffee cake, double the recipe and place the chocolate-filled

Notes:

SPRING

biscuits in a Bundt pan sprayed with nonstick cooking spray. You may need to increase the baking time slightly.

Also, use any flavor Hershey's Hugs and/or Kisses for this coffee cake.

A Spoonful of Sharing

The Bible says, "Children are a gift from the LORD; they are a reward from him" (Psalm 127:3 NLT). You are a gift to your mother and your family. What does your mother like about you? How does she show her love for you? How do you show your love for her? You could make this recipe as a gift for your mom and thank her with hugs and kisses.

Notes:

Peaches and Cream Cobbler

In this quick and easy recipe, the peaches sink down and the cake batter rises to the top. It's just right for a peach of a mom.

Difficulty: 

Prep time: 15 minutes
Baking time: 35 to 40 minutes

Gather with Grandma

½ cup (1 stick) butter
1 cup flour
½ cup sugar (plus ⅓ cup more if using fresh or unsweetened frozen peaches)
1 T. baking powder
¼ tsp. salt
⅔ cup milk
1 tsp. vanilla
3 cups sliced peaches, fresh or frozen or canned
½ tsp. cinnamon
Vanilla ice cream (optional)

Make with Grandma

1. Preheat the oven to 350°.
2. Place the butter in an ovenproof dish or baking pan (e.g., large cast-iron frying pan, deep-dish glass pie pan, or an 8-inch square cake pan). Place the pan with butter in the oven for a few minutes to melt the butter. Watch carefully so the butter doesn't burn.
3. Mix together the flour, ½ cup sugar, baking powder, and salt.
4. Add the milk and vanilla to the dry ingredients and stir.
5. Spoon the batter in small spoonfuls on top of the melted butter to cover as much of the butter as possible. Do not stir.
6. Place peach slices evenly on top of the batter.
7. If using fresh or unsweetened frozen peaches, sprinkle them with a mixture of ⅓ cup sugar and ½ teaspoon cinnamon.

Notes:

SPRING

8. If using canned sweetened peaches, drain the peaches, place them evenly on the batter and sprinkle them with only cinnamon. The batter will creep up over the peaches as it bakes.
9. Bake for 35 to 40 minutes, or until the cobbler is brown and a toothpick inserted into the cake comes out clean.
10. Serve warm with a scoop of ice cream if desired.

Makes 6 to 9 servings

Notes:

Shamrock Sundaes

Chocolate and mint make a winning combination for St. Patrick's Day or any day!

Difficulty: 

Prep time: 20 minutes
Gluten-free option: Omit the cookies or use gluten-free cookies

Gather with Grandma

8 cupcake liners
8 crisp chocolate cookies, such as Oreos
4 cups mint chocolate chip ice cream
½ cup chocolate syrup
1 to 2 cups whipped cream
8 large green gumdrops

Make with Grandma

1. Place cupcake liners in a cupcake pan.
2. Make the gumdrop shamrocks to decorate the sundaes later. With clean kitchen scissors, snip each gumdrop horizontally into 4 circles. Cut the smallest circle in half to make a stem. (Eat the other half.) Be sure to clean the sticky scissors when you're done.
3. Put the chocolate cookies in a resealable plastic bag and crush them with a rolling pin. Spoon an equal amount of crumbs into each cupcake liner.
4. Place a scoop of ice cream on top of the cookie crumbs.
5. Drizzle with chocolate syrup, and top with whipped cream.
6. Arrange three gumdrop circles on top of the whipped cream to make a shamrock (three-leaf clover). Add the stem. Serve immediately or freeze the sundaes until you're ready to eat them.

Makes 8 sundaes

Fun Fact: The shamrock, which is a symbol for Ireland and St. Patrick's Day, looks similar to a three-leaf clover. Shamrock plants have 3 heart-shaped leaves on each stem and bloom with tiny white flowers.

Summer

Sunny days, cool drinks, and relaxing vacations. A time to build sand castles, splash in the water, and enjoy picnics in the park. We can honor dads and grads, watch fireworks explode, and cultivate friendships. Fresh veggies and luscious fruits beckon us to the kitchen to make chilled soups, sandwiches, and salads for family and friends.

Taste and see that the L*ORD is good;*
blessed is the one who takes refuge in him.

PSALM 34:8

Summer

Main Dishes

Salads and Sides

Snacks

Beverages

Breads and Spreads

Desserts and Sweets

Notes:

Chicken Salad Sandwiches

Heart-shaped crustless bread filled with chicken-salad spread makes a favorite sandwich for our grade-school-aged granddaughter, Anna.

Difficulty:

Prep time: 15 minutes
Gluten-free option: Use gluten-free bread or serve the chicken salad in a cantaloupe ring or as a lettuce wrap

Gather with Grandma

2 cups cooked chicken, chopped fine (or canned, drained)
⅓ to ½ cup diced celery
⅓ cup mayonnaise (more if you prefer it moister)
2 T. plain yogurt (or milk)
Salt and pepper to taste
Sliced bread
Butter
Heart-shaped cutter
Lettuce leaves, washed

Make with Grandma

1. Mix together the chicken, celery, mayonnaise, yogurt, salt, and pepper. Chill the mixture for 30 minutes to blend flavors or until you're ready to make the sandwiches.
2. To prepare the sandwiches, cut the bread into heart shapes with a cookie cutter. Spread butter or mayonnaise on the hearts.
3. Spread on a thick layer of the chicken filling. Add a lettuce leaf and top with another heart-shaped piece of bread.
4. Wrap and refrigerate the sandwiches until you are ready to serve them. Refrigerate any leftover filling in a covered container.

Makes 2 cups filling and 8 or more heart-shaped sandwiches, depending on the size of the hearts

Notes:

Clamshell Tuna Sandwiches

A yummy catch! You won't want to clam up about these sandwiches.

Difficulty: 

Prep time: 15 minutes
Gluten-free option: Use gluten-free bread

Gather with Grandma

Large, round cookie cutter
1 (5 oz.) can tuna, drained
2 T. mayonnaise
1 T. sweet or dill pickle relish
2 T. finely chopped celery (optional)
Pepper to taste
6 slices bread
6 lettuce leaves
6 fancy toothpicks

Make with Grandma

1. In a medium-sized bowl, mix the tuna, mayonnaise, relish, celery, and pepper. (If you prefer the tuna filling to be cold, chill it for 30 minutes before serving. Otherwise, use it right away or refrigerate it until ready to serve.)
2. With a large round cookie cutter, cut each slice of bread into a 3- or 4-inch circle. (The tuna can makes a good 3-inch cutter. Or you can cut around a plastic lid with a table knife.)
3. Fold the bread circle in half, lightly creasing the center.
4. Spread 2 tablespoons filling on ½ the circle. Add a lettuce leaf.
5. Fold the bread in half to make a clamshell sandwich. Add a fancy toothpick to hold the clamshell almost shut.

Makes 4 to 6 clamshell sandwiches

Tip: My mother mashed hard-boiled eggs and mixed them with tuna for sandwiches. With many children to feed and plenty of farm-fresh eggs, Mother's tasty tuna and egg salad sandwiches eased our family budget.

Notes:

Freedom Franks in Blankets

Rally 'round the flag with these yummy treats made with cocktail-sized weiners and crescent rolls. The flag picks add a holiday touch.

Difficulty:

Prep time: 15 minutes
Baking time: 9 to 12 minutes per baking sheet

Gather with Grandma

2 (8 oz.) tubes refrigerated crescent rolls
1 (12 oz.) pkg. cocktail sausages (e.g., Lit'l Smokies)
6 1-inch cubes cheddar cheese (optional)
6 toothpick flags (optional)
Ketchup, mustard, and pickle relish
Zippy Dip, optional (see page 59)

Make with Grandma

1. Preheat the oven to 350°.
2. Separate the crescent roll dough into triangles. Cut each triangle into 3 smaller triangles using a pizza cutter.
3. Place 1 cocktail link on the wide end of each triangle. Roll the sausage and dough toward the point.
4. Place the links on the baking sheet with the pointed side of the roll down.
5. Bake for 9 to 12 minutes until the rolls are golden brown. (Bake leftover crescent rolls plain.)
6. Remove the franks from the oven and place them on a cooling rack.
7. Cut the cheese into cubes. Add a flag pick to each one.
8. To serve the Freedom Franks, place them on a serving tray. Add cheese cubes with flags on the tray for decoration.
9. Spoon favorite condiments, such as ketchup, mustard, and pickle relish, into small bowls. Make Zippy Dip to serve with them if desired.
10. Enjoy the cheese with your franks, and wave the flags.

Makes 35 Freedom Franks

Notes:

SUMMER

Grand-Slam Pulled Pork Sandwiches

These are easy to cook ahead in a Crock-Pot. Then you can heat them later for a quick, tasty meal.

Difficulty:

Prep time: 25 minutes
Cooking time: about 8 hours
Gluten-free option: Use gluten-free buns or serve over rice or potatoes

Gather with Grandma

2 or more lbs. pork shoulder or loin roast
1 (12 oz.) can root beer
1 (18 oz.) bottle favorite barbecue sauce (your favorite or KC Masterpiece original)
¼ cup water
8 sesame seed hamburger buns or Kaiser rolls

Make with Grandma

1. Place the pork roast in a Crock-Pot. Pour the root beer over the meat.
2. Cover and simmer on low for 8 hours or until the meat is fork tender and shreds easily. Halfway through cooking, turn the meat over.
3. Transfer the meat to a rimmed baking pan and let it sit until it is cool enough to handle. Using 2 forks, pull the pork into small pieces.
4. Discard the liquid from the Crock-Pot.
5. Return the pulled pork to the Crock-Pot and add the barbecue sauce.
6. Pour ¼ cup water into the empty sauce bottle. Cap it and then shake it to get the last bits of sauce. Add it to the Crock-Pot. Gently stir the sauce and pulled pork together.
7. Heat the pork on low for 30 minutes or until it's warm.
8. Spoon the barbecued pork onto warm buns and serve. Refrigerate leftovers.

Makes 8 or more servings

Notes:

SUMMER

Chilled Strawberry Soup

This cool, creamy soup tastes like a milkshake, but it is not as sweet. I first tasted it in a Washington tearoom and found it berry delicious.

Difficulty:

Prep time: 10 minutes
Chilling time: 2 to 8 hours
Gluten-free

Gather with Grandma

1 cup frozen strawberries, unsweetened (if you are using sweetened berries, omit the sugar)
1 cup milk
½ cup whipping cream
¼ cup sour cream
¼ cup powdered sugar, or to taste
¼ tsp. vanilla
Several fresh strawberries, washed (for garnish)

Make with Grandma

1. Put all the ingredients except the fresh strawberries for garnish into the blender. Blend until mixed and smooth.
2. Pour the strawberry soup into a quart jar or a covered container that holds 3 or more cups. Chill the soup for 8 hours (or at least 2). It becomes thick and creamy as it chills, but sometimes I serve it without chilling.
3. Serve the chilled soup in small bowls or teacups. Top with a slice of fresh strawberry. Refrigerate leftovers.

Makes 2½ cups

Notes:

Frosty Fruit Sparklers

Make a fun display with colorful sparklers you can eat! They add color to any picnic, especially on the Fourth of July.

Difficulty:

Prep time: 25 minutes
Gluten-free

Gather with Grandma

1 watermelon, small personal size
Red and green grapes, washed
Strawberries, washed and stemmed
Cantaloupe or honeydew melon, cut into 1-inch cubes or balls
Pineapple chunks, fresh or canned
1-inch cookie cutter, star-shaped
10-inch bamboo skewers

Make with Grandma

1. Cut the watermelon in half horizontally. Refrigerate one half to use later.
2. Cut the other half into ¾-inch slices. Use cookie cutter to cut the slices into shapes, such as stars.
3. Thread a variety of fruit on the skewers, alternating shapes and colors. Make at least 1 sparkler per person.
4. Serve the fruit kabobs fresh or freeze them for several hours first. If you freeze them, remove them from the freezer 5 to 10 minutes before serving.
5. To serve the sparklers, place the remaining half watermelon on a plate or tray with the cut side down. Poke the sparklers into the melon to create a colorful display. It makes a fun centerpiece for any summer event. Refrigerate leftover fruit.

Serves as many as you wish to make

Notes:

Honeydew Canoes

Keep your boat afloat and then eat it. My youngest granddaughter likes grapes and puts more than one "grape person" in her canoe.

Difficulty:

Prep time: 10 minutes
Gluten-free

Gather with Grandma

½ honeydew melon (or cantaloupe)
12 green grapes, washed
12 red grapes, washed
Toothpicks
1 peeled carrot for oars (or use pretzel sticks)

Make with Grandma

1. Cut the melon in half. Remove the seeds.
2. Cut one melon half into 4 to 6 wedges to make canoes.
3. Stick 1 green and 1 red grape on a toothpick to make a person's head and body. Poke the toothpick into the melon canoe.
4. Cut the carrots into small strips to use as oars. With a toothpick, poke a hole into each side of the melon slice by the "grape person." Place a carrot-strip oar into each hole. (Pretzel sticks also work as oars, but they become soggy quickly.)
5. Row, row, row your boat. Then eat this healthy treat.

Makes 4 to 6 canoes

A Spoonful of Sharing

As you eat your canoe, read about the time Jesus's disciples were caught in a big storm on a lake. They were afraid they would drown! But the story has a happy ending. "Even the winds and the waves obey him!" (Mark 4:41). You can read the story in Mark 4:35-41 or Luke 8:22-25. What can we learn from this story?

SUMMER

Notes:

SUMMER

Out-of-the-Park Cheesy Potatoes

Covered with baked potato toppings, this recipe is a winner.

Difficulty:

Prep time: 30 minutes
Baking time: 50 to 60 minutes
Gluten-free

Gather with Grandma

Potatoes

1 (26 to 32 oz.) package diced hash brown potatoes, thawed
1½ cups milk
½ cup mayonnaise
2 T. cornstarch
½ tsp. salt
¼ tsp. pepper
1 tsp. dill weed (optional)

Potato Toppings

1 cup sour cream
1½ cups sharp cheddar cheese, grated
½ cup crumbled bacon bits (about 4 slices cooked crisp)
2 green onions, sliced (optional)

Make with Grandma

1. Preheat the oven to 350°. Spray a 9 x 13-inch pan with nonstick cooking spray.
2. Spread the potatoes in the baking pan.
3. In a bowl, whisk together the milk, mayonnaise, and cornstarch.
4. Add the salt, pepper, and dill to the milk mixture.
5. Pour the mixture over the potatoes and stir until the potatoes are coated.
6. Spread the potato mixture evenly in the pan.
7. Using a rubber spatula, carefully spread the sour cream over the potatoes.

Notes:

8. Top the potatoes with cheese, bacon, and green onions.
9. Bake the potatoes uncovered for 50 to 60 minutes, until the potatoes bubble and are soft when poked with a fork.
10. Remove the potatoes from the oven and place the pan on a cooling rack. The sauce on the potatoes will thicken as they cool. Refrigerate leftovers.

Serves 8 to 10 people

Variations: For a crunchy topping, sprinkle 1 cup crushed potato chips on top of the potatoes just before serving.

For a main dish, add 2 cups cubed ham to the potatoes before baking.

Tip: You can prepare this recipe ahead of time. Cover the unbaked potatoes and refrigerate them overnight or until you're ready to bake them. Bake uncovered.

Notes:

SUMMER

Seashell Pasta Salad

You can't listen to the ocean in these shells, but eating them will remind you of the beach.

Difficulty:

Prep time: 20 minutes
Chilling time: 3 hours
Gluten-free option: Use gluten-free pasta

Gather with Grandma

1 cup small shell pasta, uncooked
1 cup medium shell pasta, uncooked
1 cup peas, frozen (optional)
½ cup black olives, sliced (so they look like inner tubes)
½ cup cherry tomatoes (optional)
⅓ cup pepperoni, sliced thin and cut in strips
2 T. Parmesan cheese, shredded
⅓ to ½ cup Italian salad dressing
Parsley, cherry tomatoes, and olives for garnish
A clean plastic sand bucket and shovel for serving

Make with Grandma

1. Cook the two pastas according to the package directions (about 10 minutes).
2. Drain the pasta in a colander and rinse it with cold water.
3. Refrigerate the pasta for 1 hour or until chilled.
4. To thaw the frozen peas, put them into a sieve, and rinse them with warm water.
5. Add the peas, olives, cherry tomatoes, pepperoni, Parmesan cheese, and dressing to the chilled pasta. Stir to combine.
6. Chill the salad for at least 2 hours to blend the flavors.
7. For fun, serve the salad in a small bucket lined with foil. Serve with the sand shovel or a large spoon. Garnish the salad with cherry tomatoes and parsley in the center and a few olives around the edge.

Makes about 5 cups

Notes:

A Spoonful of Sharing

What do you like to do at the beach? Have you ever tried counting the grains of sand? In the Bible, David compares the grains of sand to God's love for us. "How precious are your thoughts about me, O God. They cannot be numbered! I can't even count them; they outnumber the grains of sand! And when I wake up, you are still with me!" (Psalm 139:17-18 NLT). Just as sand covers the beach, God's loving presence surrounds us all the time.

Notes:

SUMMER

Triple Play Bean Salad

Easy to make, colorful, and flavorful. A tasty addition to a summer picnic or meal.

Difficulty:

Prep time: 10 minutes
Chilling time: 2 hours or longer
Gluten-free

Gather with Grandma

Salad

1 (15 oz.) can green beans
1 (15 oz.) can yellow wax beans
1 (15 oz.) can dark red kidney beans
2 T. chopped onion

Dressing

⅓ to ½ cup granulated sugar (to taste)
⅓ cup white vinegar
¼ cup salad oil
¼ tsp. black pepper

Make with Grandma

1. Pour each can of beans into a colander to drain the liquid. Rinse them with water.
2. Mix the beans and onion in a large bowl.
3. In another bowl, whisk together the sugar, vinegar, oil, and pepper.
4. Pour the dressing over the beans and stir them together.
5. Cover the salad and let it marinate in the refrigerator for at least 2 hours.

Makes 4½ cups

Variation: Add one (15 oz.) can garbanzo beans for extra protein.

Notes:

Zippy Dip

Add some zip to your meal with this quick, easy, and delicious dip. It tastes yummy with Freedom Franks in Blankets (see page 49).

Difficulty:

Prep time: 5 minutes
Gluten-free

Gather with Grandma

¼ cup sour cream
¼ cup mayonnaise
1 T. Dijon mustard

Make with Grandma

1. Whisk the ingredients together.
2. Chill the dip until ready to use.
3. Refrigerate leftovers in a covered container.

Makes ½ cup dip

Notes:

SUMMER

Goin' Fishin' Snack Mix

Salty like the ocean breeze and sweet to please!

Difficulty:

Prep time: 20 minutes

Gather with Grandma

2 cups fish crackers (original flavor)
2 cups pretzel sticks (for fishing poles)
2 cups crisp cereal squares, such as Chex
½ cup peanuts or mixed nuts (optional)
¼ cup (½ stick) butter or margarine
¼ cup plus 2 T. packed brown sugar
2 T. light corn syrup
½ tsp. vanilla

Make with Grandma

1. In a large microwave-safe bowl, combine the crackers, pretzels, cereal, and peanuts.
2. In a medium-sized microwave-safe bowl, combine the butter, sugar, corn syrup, and vanilla. Cover and microwave the mixture on medium for 1 minute. Stir. (Be careful—the mixture will be hot.)
3. Microwave the butter-sugar mixture for another minute or until the butter melts and the mixture boils. Stir well.
4. Carefully pour the butter-sugar mixture over the cracker mixture. Stir with a wooden spoon until the snack mix is evenly coated.
5. Microwave the mix on high for 2 minutes and stir. Microwave at medium power for 2 to 3 additional minutes, stirring every 1 to 2 minutes. Be careful not to overcook the mixture and burn it.
6. Spread the mixture on wax paper to cool.
7. Nibble on your fishy catch. Store leftovers in an airtight container or plastic bag.

Makes 6 cups

Notes:

Patriotic Punch

Enjoy this cool drink on a hot day. Colorful ice cubes create a patriotic splash. My grandkids like this fun idea for a refreshing punch. It's extra special served on the Fourth of July.

Difficulty:

Prep time: 10 minutes
Freezing time: 2 hours
Gluten-free

Gather with Grandma

3 ice cube trays or 3 mini muffin pans
Red beverage, such as Kool-Aid, fruit juice, or punch
Blue beverage, such as Powerade; or use blue food coloring to tint lemonade, white grape juice, or clear soda
2-liter bottle lemon-lime or other clear soda
Clear drinking glasses
Red straws (optional)

Make with Grandma

1. Fill one ice cube tray with the red beverage, another with the clear soda, and the third with a blue beverage. Freeze the cubes until solid. Chill the leftover beverages.
2. When you're ready to serve the punch, remove the ice cubes from the freezer and place 1 ice cube of each color in each glass, or place several of each color in a glass pitcher. Place the remaining punch cubes in 3 separate bags and store them in the freezer.
3. Pour clear soda over the ice cubes to cover them. Add a straw to individual glasses and enjoy this refreshing drink!
4. As the ice melts, watch for colored bubbles. Eventually, the punch may change color.

Serves 4 to 6

Note: As the ice cubes melt, the flavors will mix together. Select beverages that will taste good blended.

Notes:

SUMMER

Tip: If you make one color ice cubes with a sugared beverage and another with an artificially sweetened beverage, place the heavier cubes (beverage with sugar) on the bottom. Then the colors will layer as the ice melts.

A Spoonful of Sharing

As you watch the red, white, and blue ice cubes in your punch melt, thank God for America's godly heritage. Do you know that our money shows what our nation believes? Examine coins and paper bills and find "In God We Trust" on each one. Then read Proverbs 3:5-6 and talk about why we can trust God.

Notes:

Luscious Lemon Curd

Lemon curd is a favorite with my grandkids. It tastes like lemon pie filling.

Difficulty:

Prep time: 35 minutes
Gluten-free

Gather with Grandma

1 large fresh lemon (squeeze for juice—you will need ½ cup—and save peel for zest)
Bottled lemon juice (if needed to make ½ cup lemon juice total)
1¼ cups granulated sugar
2 T. cornstarch
¼ cup water
3 large eggs (¾ cup)
¼ cup (½ stick) butter, cut into small pieces
1 T. lemon zest, made from finely grated fresh lemon peel

Make with Grandma

1. Roll the lemon on the counter so it will be easier to squeeze out the juice.
2. Grate the peel from the lemon. Set aside 1 tablespoon grated zest, or less if the lemon doesn't yield that much.
3. Cut the lemon in half and squeeze out the juice. Strain out the seeds and measure the juice. You will probably need more juice to fill ½ cup. Add bottled lemon juice for the rest or squeeze juice from another fresh lemon.
4. Combine the sugar and cornstarch in a 1- or 2-quart saucepan. Stir in the lemon juice and water.
5. In a separate bowl, thoroughly beat the eggs until lemon colored. Set them aside.
6. Cook the sugar mixture in the saucepan over medium heat, stirring with a wooden spoon until it comes to a boil. Then cook for 1 minute, stirring constantly. Cool slightly.
7. Pour a small amount of the mixture from the saucepan into the beaten

Notes:

eggs, stirring until blended. Then add that egg mixture back to the rest of the sauce in the saucepan.

8. Stirring constantly, continue cooking over medium heat until the mixture comes to a boil. Reduce the heat and cook for 1 minute.
9. Remove the pan from the heat and add the butter and lemon zest. Stir until the butter is melted and the curd is smooth and creamy. Refrigerate the curd in a covered container until ready to serve.
10. Serve on scones, toast, waffles, and pancakes. Refrigerate leftovers (if you have any). The curd keeps in the refrigerator for 1 or 2 weeks.

Makes 2 cups

Notes:

Scone Blossoms

Sugar cubes give these blossoms a sweet center. My grandkids like to push in the sugar cubes and eat one as they help. The cream in the recipe replaces the butter or shortening that scone recipes often include. *(Inspired by a recipe from Grammy Becky.)*

Difficulty:

Prep time: 25 minutes
Baking time: 12 to 15 minutes

Gather with Grandma

2 cups flour
¼ cup granulated sugar
1 T. baking powder
½ tsp. salt
1¼ cups whipping cream, unwhipped
½ tsp. vanilla
1 T. orange juice concentrate (not diluted with water)
14 sugar cubes
2½-inch flower-shaped cookie cutter
1 T. powdered sugar (optional)

Make with Grandma

1. Preheat the oven to 400°. Lightly grease a baking sheet with nonstick cooking spray.
2. In a large bowl, mix together the flour, sugar, baking powder, and salt.
3. Add the whipping cream and vanilla and mix.
4. On a lightly floured surface, knead the dough gently until combined. If it is too dry, add another tablespoon of cream.
5. Roll the dough ½ inch thick. Cut the dough into about 14 blossoms. If you don't have a flower cookie cutter, cut the scones into 2½-inch circles. Then make ½-inch snips around the edge of the circle to make petals.
6. Mix the undiluted orange juice with 1 teaspoon water. Dip each sugar cube into the juice and push 1 cube into the center of each scone.

Notes:

7. Bake the scones for 12 to 15 minutes or until lightly browned. (Some of the sugary center may bubble out, but that's all right.)
8. Remove the scones from the oven and cool them on a cooling rack. Lightly dust them with powdered sugar if desired.
9. Serve the scones warm with lemon curd and Homemade Whipped Cream (see page 38) or jam, honey, and butter.

Makes 14 scones

A Spoonful of Sharing

As you eat these Scone Blossoms, talk about the joy of friends and how to make friendships blossom. Proverbs 17:17 says, "A friend loves at all times." How can you be a good friend? What makes your friends special? Would you like to invite someone over for scones?

Notes:

Batter Balls

Batter up! Everyone will love these balls of edible chocolate chip cookie dough. Make them as a Father's Day gift to let Dad know he's on the ball. You can also dip these balls into chocolate and turn them into truffles, but my son and grandkids are just as happy to eat the dough with a spoon. (*From the kitchen of Grandma Kathleen in New Hampshire.)*

Difficulty: for balls 🥄 / for truffles 🥄🥄

Prep time to mix: 15 minutes
Time to dip truffles: 45 minutes

Gather with Grandma

½ cup (1 stick) softened butter
¾ cup brown sugar, firmly packed
1 tsp. vanilla
1 (14 oz.) can sweetened condensed milk
2 cups flour, heated before using (see the note below)
¾ cup miniature semisweet chocolate chips
½ cup chopped walnuts or pecans (optional)
1 (12 oz.) package dark chocolate chips, melted (optional)
Extra mini chips and sprinkles for decorating (optional)

Make with Grandma

1. Cream together the butter, sugar, and vanilla until fluffy.
2. Mix in the condensed milk. Add the flour a little at a time and mix well. (You may want to mix it with your hands.)
3. Mix in the chips and nuts. The dough is now ready to eat. You can refrigerate it in a covered container or roll it into balls.
4. For truffles, shape the dough into 1-inch balls. Place them on baking sheets lined with wax paper. Refrigerate them for 1 or 2 hours to become firm.
5. To dip them, melt the chocolate chips in the microwave following the package directions. I melt about ⅓ cup chips at a time in a custard cup.
6. Place balls into the melted chocolate 1 at a time. Coat them by turning them in the chocolate with a fork. Then use two forks, one in each hand, to remove the balls, letting the excess chocolate drip off before placing the balls

Notes:

on the wax paper–lined cookie sheet. Top each one with a few mini chocolate chips, sprinkles, or nuts, if desired.

7. Chill the truffles in the refrigerator until the chocolate is firm.
8. Place the truffles in a covered container and keep them refrigerated until you are ready to serve them or give them as a gift. Keep leftover truffles or batter balls refrigerated.

Note: Eating raw flour can be harmful, so it is recommended to heat the flour first. Preheat the oven to 350°. Place 2 cups flour in a 9 x 13-inch pan and bake it for 5 minutes. Cool completely. Then sift and use.

Makes 3 dozen balls or truffles

A Spoonful of Sharing

Many dads like baseball and other sports. As you stir up these Batter Balls, share what your dad likes to do. What do you like to do with him? Father's Day and every day is a great time to love and honor your dad.

Notes:

Fluffy Frosting

Creamy and quick to make. It's scrumptious on cakes, shortcake, or any recipe that calls for frosting or whipped cream.

Difficulty: 

Prep time: 15 minutes

Gather with Grandma

- 1 (4-serving size) box instant vanilla pudding
- 1 cup milk
- 2 cups frozen whipped topping, thawed (use extra creamy if available)

Make with Grandma

1. Whisk together the pudding and milk until well blended. It will be soft set in five minutes.
2. Fold in the whipped topping.
3. Chill the frosting in a covered container until ready to serve. Refrigerate leftovers.

Makes 3 cups frosting

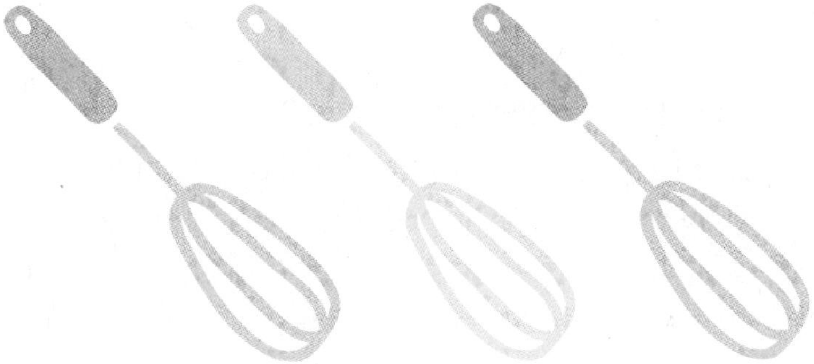

SUMMER

Notes:

SUMMER

Root Beer Float Cookie Sandwiches

Turn these crisp cookies that melt in your mouth into an ice cream sandwich. They will remind you of a root beer float.

Difficulty:

Prep time: 50 minutes
Making cookie sandwiches: 20 minutes

Gather with Grandma

1 cup (2 sticks) butter, softened
½ cup granulated sugar
½ cup brown sugar
1 egg
1 T. root beer concentrate or extract
2 cups plus 2 T. flour
½ tsp. baking soda
¼ tsp. salt
½ gallon vanilla ice cream

Make with Grandma

1. Preheat the oven to 350°. Spray a cookie sheet with nonstick cooking spray or use parchment paper.
2. Cream together the butter and sugars until fluffy.
3. Mix in the egg and root beer concentrate.
4. Add the flour, baking soda, and salt. Mix well.
5. Form the dough into 1-inch balls and place them on a prepared cookie sheet.
6. Dip a flat-bottomed glass into extra sugar and press it down on the cookie ball. Dip the glass in the sugar a second time and stamp the cookie to leave some sugar on top.
7. Bake the cookies for 10 minutes or until they are lightly browned around the edges.
8. Remove the cookies from the baking sheet and cool them on a rack. (The cookies taste delicious plain.)

9. To make them into ice cream sandwiches, use a small scoop (about ¼ cup) of ice cream for each sandwich. Place the ice cream between two pieces of wax paper and flatten it by pressing it with your hand. Remove the paper and place the ice cream between two cookies. Eat the sandwiches immediately or freeze them for later.

Makes 36 cookies for 18 ice cream sandwiches

Variation: For creamsicle sandwiches, replace the root beer extract with 1 teaspoon orange extract. Tint the dough orange (combine yellow and red food colors if you don't have orange) if desired. When flattening the cookies, dip the glass into granulated sugar or orange sugar sprinkles. Eat the cookies plain or make ice cream sandwiches, which taste a little like eating a creamsicle.

Notes:

Notes:

SUMMER

Sandbar Surprises

A cool ice cream treat with a hidden surprise.

Difficulty:

Prep time: 30 minutes

Gather with Grandma

½ gallon ice cream (vanilla or a flavor you like)
Blue food coloring
24 vanilla wafers (1 cup crushed wafers)
9 Swedish Fish candies
9 paper umbrella picks

Make with Grandma

1. Slightly thaw the ice cream. If using a white ice cream, add 2 or 3 drops blue food coloring into the softened ice cream.
2. Put the vanilla wafers into a quart-sized, sealable plastic bag. Crush the wafers into "sand" by pounding them with a rolling pin.
3. Scoop the softened ice cream into an 8-inch square pan and smooth it.
4. Press the Swedish fish into the ice cream as a buried surprise. Put 3 across in 3 rows so 1 fish is hidden in each of the 9 servings.
5. Sprinkle cookie crumb "sand" over the top of the ice cream. Gently pat the "sand" down. Then freeze the sandbars for 1 hour or until firm.
6. To serve, cut the sandbars into 9 squares. Top each square with a paper umbrella poked in diagonally to look like a beach umbrella.

Serves 9

A Spoonful of Sharing

While eating Sandbar Surprises, talk about the foolish man who built his house on the sand and how we can be wise (Matthew 7:24-29). Wisdom is making smart choices that please God. See Proverbs 2:1-7 (NLT) for ideas on how to be wise.

Notes:

Show Your Colors Cupcakes

Top these cupcakes with the colors of your flag. Then fly toothpick flags on them and thank God for your freedom.

Difficulty:

Prep time: 20 minutes
Baking time: 25 minutes

Gather with Grandma

1 (15.25 oz.) package Funfetti cake mix or cake mix of your choice
Fresh strawberries, sliced
Fresh blueberries, washed
Flaked coconut
Small flag picks or candles for decoration
Vanilla ice cream (optional)

Make with Grandma

1. Preheat the oven according to the package directions and prepare 2 cupcake pans with paper liners.
2. Make cupcakes according to package instructions and bake as directed. Let cool.
3. Have on hand a ready-made vanilla frosting or prepare Fluffy Frosting (see page 69). You can make it a few hours ahead, cover, and refrigerate.
4. When you're ready to serve this dessert, fill separate serving bowls with strawberries, blueberries, and coconut.
5. Place the cupcakes, frosting, toppings, and flag picks on the table and let each person frost and decorate his or her own cupcake. If you include ice cream, serve the cupcakes in bowls.

Makes 2 dozen cupcakes

Notes:

SUMMER

Triple Treat Triangles

What could be better than brownies, chocolate chip cookies, and chocolate candies all in one bar? This decadent cookie is easy to prepare using cookie mixes.

Difficulty:

Prep time: 25 minutes
Baking time: 25 to 30 minutes

Gather with Grandma

1 (18.3 oz.) package fudge brownie mix
1 (7.5 oz.) package chocolate chip cookie mix
½ cup mini M&M's

Make with Grandma

1. Preheat the oven to 350°. Spray a 9 x 13-inch baking pan with nonstick cooking spray.
2. Prepare the brownie mix according to the package directions. Spread the batter in the pan.
3. Mix together the chocolate chip cookies according to the package directions. Drop the dough by small teaspoonfuls on top of the brownie batter.
4. Sprinkle the mini M&M's on top of the cookies.
5. Bake according to the directions for the brownies. Brownies are done when a toothpick inserted 1 inch from the edge of the pan comes out clean. You may need to increase the baking time by 5 or 10 minutes. Watch carefully.
6. When done, remove the pan from the oven and place it on a cooling rack. Let the cookies cool completely before cutting.
7. Cut the cookies into 2-inch squares. Then cut each square diagonally to form triangles. Serve them in individual paper liners if desired.

Makes about 3 dozen triangles

Variation: Replace the chocolate chip cookie mix with a (7.2 oz.) package of peanut butter cookie mix. Delicious!

Fall

Back to school, jumping in golden leaves, carving pumpkins, and counting our blessings. Let's celebrate Grandparents Day, fall fun, Thanksgiving, and perhaps do a little stargazing on a clear night. It's also a great season to cook with apples, cranberries, and pumpkin.

Let them give thanks to the L*ORD*...*for he satisfies the thirsty and fills the hungry with good things.*

PSALM 107:8-9

Fall

Main Dishes

Salads and Sides

Snacks

Breads

Desserts and Sweets

Notes:

A-Maze-ing Corn Chowder with Sausage

Corn mazes are a popular fall activity in some areas. But even if you don't go through a maze, you'll love this a-maze-ing corn chowder.

Difficulty:

Prep time: 25 minutes
Gluten-free

Gather with Grandma

1 lb. sweet Italian sausage
1 small onion, chopped (about ½ cup)
4 cups frozen hash brown potatoes, thawed (country-style, cubed)
1 cup water
½ tsp. salt
Pepper to taste
1 (15.25 oz.) can whole-kernel corn with liquid
1 (14.75 oz.) can cream-style corn
1 (12 oz.) can evaporated milk (or substitute 1 cup cream)

Make with Grandma

1. If the sausage is only available in links, remove the casing. Fry the sausage and onion together until the sausage is brown and the onion is tender (5 to 10 minutes).
2. If needed, drain the sausage mixture on a paper towel to get rid of the excess grease.
3. Transfer the sausage mixture to a 6-quart saucepan. Add the potatoes, water, salt, and pepper. Bring the chowder to a boil, and then reduce the heat and simmer the mixture just until the potatoes are tender, about 3 minutes.
4. Stir in both kinds of corn and evaporated milk.
5. Bring the soup to a boil. Immediately reduce the temperature and simmer the soup on low to heat it through. Enjoy. Refrigerate leftovers.

Makes 9 cups

Notes:

Build-Your-Bear Sandwiches

These sandwiches taste delicious and are un-bearably cute.

Difficulty:

Prep time: 20 minutes
Gluten-free option: Use gluten-free bread and meat

Gather with Grandma

Teddy bear cookie cutter (3 inches tall)
8 slices wheat bread
4 thin slices ham (easier to cut if thin sliced)
4 slices cheddar cheese
4 lettuce leaves
Mayonnaise or ranch dressing
Mustard
Butter
1 red bell pepper or jellied cranberry sauce to make a heart for a garnish (optional)

See page 148 for Ranch Dressing and Dip.

Make with Grandma

1. Cut the bread, ham, and cheese slices with the cookie cutter.
2. Spread mayonnaise and/or mustard on 4 pieces of bear-shaped bread.
3. Top each slice of bread with ham, cheese, and lettuce.
4. Butter the other 4 bear shapes and put them on top of the sandwiches.
5. If desired, use a small heart-shaped cutter to cut a heart from a red bell pepper or from a slice of jellied cranberry sauce. Place the heart on top of the sandwich.
6. Enjoy your tasty bear sandwiches.

Makes 4 sandwiches

Notes:

Mac 'n' Cheese Cups

Easy, cheesy, creamy comfort food. My taste testers called it "super yummy." Grandma Dianna said, "It's tasty, a nice consistency, and easy to make."

Difficulty:

Prep time: 25 minutes
Gluten-free option: Use gluten-free pasta and breadcrumbs, or omit breadcrumbs

Gather with Grandma

2½ cups milk
2 cups elbow macaroni (or medium-sized shells)
1 T. butter
½ tsp. salt
4 oz. cream cheese, softened (about ½ cup)
½ tsp. dry mustard (optional)
Dash of black pepper (optional)
6 oz. extra-sharp cheddar cheese or white cheddar, grated (about 2 cups)
½ cup crushed croutons (optional)

Make with Grandma

1. Pour the milk into a 3-quart saucepan.
2. Rinse the macaroni in water and drain it. This reduces the starch.
3. Add the macaroni, butter, and salt to the milk. Cook the macaroni on medium heat for the suggested cooking time on the package. Stir the mixture frequently with a wooden spoon to keep it from scorching on the bottom of the pan.
4. When the macaroni is soft but not mushy, add the cream cheese and stir it until the cheese melts. Mix in the dry mustard and pepper if you wish.
5. Turn off the heat and add the cheddar cheese. Stir the mixture until the cheese is melted and well blended. The macaroni is now ready to eat or to make into Mac 'n' Cheese Cups.
6. For Mac 'n' Cheese Cups, spoon the macaroni into individual ½ cup or larger ramekins or custard cups. Sprinkle crushed croutons on top of each

Notes:

serving. If needed, cover the individual servings and heat them in the microwave on medium until they are piping hot.

7. Refrigerate the leftovers. But don't be surprised if there aren't any.

Makes 4 cups

Tip: For best results, use a block of cheddar cheese and grate it yourself instead of buying preshredded cheese. It will melt faster and taste creamier that way. Packaged shredded cheese often has a coating to keep shreds from sticking together. Also, the cream cheese in the recipe makes the Mac 'n' Cheese creamy without changing the flavor.

FALL

Notes:

Meat-eor Bites

You'll lick your lips when you bite into these out-of-this-world meatballs. My daughter-in-law named them after meteorites because they are bites of meat with rice sticking out, which gives them an unusual look.

Difficulty: 🥄🥄🥄

Prep time: 20 minutes
Cooking time: 30 to 40 minutes
Gluten-free: Use gluten-free Worcestershire sauce

Gather with Grandma

Meatballs

- 1 lb. lean ground beef
- ½ cup water
- ½ cup long-grain rice, uncooked
- 2 T. minced dried onion
- 1 T. fresh parsley, snipped
- 1 tsp. salt
- ⅛ tsp. pepper
- ¼ tsp. garlic powder or to taste
- 2 T. oil

Sauce

- 1 (15 oz.) can tomato sauce
- 1 cup water
- 3 T. brown sugar
- 1 tsp. Worcestershire sauce

Make with Grandma

1. In a large bowl combine the ground beef, ½ cup water, rice, onion, parsley, salt, pepper, and garlic. Shape the mixture into about 24 to 30 1-inch meatballs.
2. Add oil to the skillet and heat it on medium. Add meatballs and brown them on all sides. Be careful—the water in the meatballs may combine with the oil in the pan and splatter. If the meatballs stick, add nonstick cooking spray.

FALL

Notes:

3. When the meatballs are brown, drain the excess grease.
4. To make the sauce, combine the tomato sauce, water, sugar, and Worcestershire sauce.
5. Pour the sauce over the meatballs and cover the pan with a lid.
6. Simmer the meatballs and sauce for 30 to 40 minutes or until the rice is tender. If needed, add a few tablespoons of water to keep the meatballs moist so the rice cooks completely.
7. Serve the Meat-eor Bites warm with toothpicks as an appetizer. They also make a satisfying main dish of meat, rice, and sauce. Refrigerate the leftovers. They make tasty sandwiches.

Makes 24 or more 1-inch Meat-eor Bites

Notes:

Solar Eclipse Toast

A fun way to eat eggs and toast. Create your own eclipse by placing the circle of bread on top of the sun (egg).

Difficulty:

Prep time: 10 minutes
Gluten-free option: Use gluten-free bread

Gather with Grandma (for 1 serving)

2-inch round cookie cutter
1 large slice bread
1 T. butter
1 egg
Salt and pepper

Make with Grandma

1. Place a slice of bread on a plate. Lightly butter both sides of the bread.
2. Cut a circle from the center of the bread with a cookie cutter.
3. Warm the skillet and spray it with nonstick cooking spray. Place the slice of bread and separate circle in the skillet. Add butter inside the hole in the bread.
4. For an over-easy egg, crack the egg into a small dish and pour it into the open circle in the bread. Lightly sprinkle the egg with salt and pepper. Turn over to brown both sides of the bread.
5. For a sunny-side-up egg, brown the bread on one side, turn it over, and then add the butter and egg in the circle. Cook the egg on medium heat until done. Brown the bread circle on both sides.
6. To serve, cover the egg completely with the bread circle to make a total eclipse. Move the circle over the egg halfway for a partial eclipse.

Make as many servings as needed

Variation: Spray a baking pan generously with nonstick cooking spray. Bake the egg and toast in the oven at 400° for 8 to 15 minutes or until the egg is cooked as you prefer. If desired, sprinkle grated cheese on top of the egg before baking.

Notes:

FALL

A Spoonful of Sharing

One night when the moon was bright, my grandkids ran outside with me. Clara looked up to the night sky and asked, "Who owns the moon?"

"God does," I said. "He made it."

"Oh, I thought we did since we landed on the moon first," Clara said.

I understood what she meant. But the Bible gives this answer in Isaiah 40:26:

"Lift up your eyes and look to the heavens: Who created all these? He who brings out the starry host one by one and calls forth each of them by name. Because of his great power and mighty strength, not one of them is missing."

Search online for photos or videos to learn more about eclipses and God's amazing starry creation. Also, these Bible verses talk about the sun, moon, and stars (Genesis 1:16; Psalm 147:4; Psalm 8:3-4).

Notes:

Frosty Cranberry Circles

This salad is yummy enough to serve as a dessert!

Difficulty:

Prep time: 30 minutes
Freezing time: 4 hours
Gluten-free

Gather with Grandma

1 (8 oz.) pkg. cream cheese, softened
1 (16 oz.) can whole-berry cranberry sauce
1 T. mayonnaise
1 (8 oz.) can crushed pineapple, drained
1 cup whipped cream (½ cup unwhipped)
½ cup chopped walnuts (optional)
Lettuce leaves

Make with Grandma

1. Place the cream cheese in a large mixing bowl and beat it for 1 minute or until fluffy.
2. Add the cranberry sauce and mayonnaise, and then beat the mixture together until blended.
3. Stir in the drained pineapple.
4. Fold in the whipped cream. Add nuts if desired.
5. Spoon the salad mixture into paper cups or empty cranberry and crushed pineapple cans. Cover the salad with plastic wrap and secure it with rubber bands. Freeze the containers standing upright for at least 4 hours, until solid.
6. Remove the salad from the paper cups or cans and slice it into ¾-inch circles. Serve each slice on a lettuce leaf.

Serves 10

Notes:

Fruity Turkey Favors

My husband and I created these turkeys together at the dinner table. I got a mandarin orange from the fridge, and Milt took out the last few grapes. "Don't eat the grapes," I said. "I think we can make a turkey from them." So we did.

Difficulty: 🥄

Prep time: 15 minutes to make 2
Gluten-free

Gather with Grandma

Tangerines or small oranges, unpeeled
Red and green grapes
Raisins and Craisins
Toothpicks

Make with Grandma

1. Place an unpeeled tangerine or orange on a small plate.
2. Alternate 2 or 3 red and green grapes on toothpicks to make tail feathers. On some toothpicks, put the red grapes on top and green grapes on top of others. Use 5 toothpicks with grapes for the tail feathers on each tangerine.
3. Poke the "tail feathers" into the top of the orange at an angle. (If you put them too far back, the turkey will tip backward.)
4. Put 2 raisins onto a toothpick for a neck. Add a green grape for the head, leaving a bit of toothpick sticking out through the grape for the beak. Attach the "neck" to the front of the orange.
5. Shape a Craisin, making it long and thin for a wattle. Poke it onto the toothpick "beak" on the grape "head."

Make 1 fruity turkey favor for each person to gobble up!

Notes:

A Spoonful of Sharing

Turkeys remind us of Thanksgiving. What are the two words in Thanksgiving? What does the word become if you reverse the two words? The Bible includes many verses about giving thanks. Here's one: "In everything give thanks; for this is God's will for you in Christ Jesus" (1 Thessalonians 5:18 NASB). Share things you are thankful for.

Notes:

Veggie Wagons

Build a wagon and load it with your favorite fresh veggies or dried fruits and nuts. Then it will deliver healthy foods to you.

Difficulty:

Prep time: 15 minutes
Gluten-free

Gather with Grandma

Celery stalks, washed
Whole peeled carrot (about 1 inch thick)
Cream cheese, hummus, or peanut butter
Toothpicks
Black or green olives, cut in half crosswise (optional)
Fresh veggies, such as peas, diced carrots, broccoli, or radishes (optional)
Dried fruit, such as raisins, Craisins, apricots, or pineapple (optional)
Nuts (optional)

Make with Grandma

1. Cut the celery stalks crosswise into 2½-inch lengths for the wagon beds.
2. Fill the celery wagon with 1 teaspoonful of cream cheese, hummus, or peanut butter.
3. Cut the carrot into ¼-inch thick circles to make wheels (4 per wagon).
4. Push a toothpick into the center of a carrot wheel. Add another carrot wheel on the other end. Repeat to make 2 sets of wheels. If desired, add olive slices outside the wheels for hubcaps.
5. Arrange the wheels 1½ inches apart on a plate.
6. Place the filled celery wagon between the wheels to rest on the toothpicks.
7. Cut a thin, 2-inch strip of carrot or celery for the wagon handle. Poke the handle into the celery filling at an angle.
8. If desired, load your wagon with bits of vegetables, dried fruit, or nuts.

Make as many as needed

Notes:

Blast Off Rocket Snack

Launch into space with this delicious popcorn, cheese, and apple snack. Three... two...one... Zoom to the moon!

Difficulty:

Prep time 20 minutes
Gluten-free

Gather with Grandma (for each rocket)

1 apple
1 mozzarella cheese stick
1 cup popped popcorn (or more if desired)
Peanut butter or whipped cream cheese
Sliced cheddar cheese
Toothpick

Make with Grandma

1. Cut the apple in half vertically from the stem down and remove the core. Use half an apple for the launching pad. Cut 3 thin apple slices from the other half of the apple for the rocket fins and a crescent moon.
2. Place the half apple with the cut side down on a medium-sized plate.
3. Trim the top of the cheese stick to make a point.
4. Use a toothpick to attach the bottom of the cheese stick to the apple, leaving a ½ inch space between the cheese and apple so the toothpick shows. Now the rocket stands up. Make a small slit on each side of the cheese stick, about 3 inches from the point. Cut 2 apple slices shorter (about 2 inches long) and use them as "fins." Push the fins into the slits in the cheese stick.
5. Use peanut butter or whipped cream cheese to glue popcorn at the bottom of the cheese stick and on top of the apple for rocket "exhaust." Scatter the rest of the popcorn exhaust on the plate.
6. Cut cheddar cheese stars with a small star-shaped cutter. Place stars on the plate to make a galaxy. Add an apple slice for a crescent-shaped moon.

Notes:

Pumpkin Patch Cheese Balls

In the fall, it's fun to go to a pumpkin farm and pick your own pumpkin from the field. Even if you don't, you can pick your pumpkin-shaped cheese ball from this patch.

Difficulty:

Prep time: 20 minutes
Chilling time: 2 hours
Gluten-free option: Use gluten-free pretzels and Worcestershire sauce

Gather with Grandma

8 oz. cream cheese, softened
8 oz. garden vegetable cream cheese spread
1½ cups sharp cheddar cheese, finely grated, divided
1 small orange bell pepper (you will only use the stem)
Pretzel sticks
Celery leaves
Rubber bands, for larger pumpkins

Make with Grandma

1. Combine the cream cheese, cream cheese spread, and ¾ cup cheddar cheese. Mix well.
2. Shape the mixture into 1 large ball, 2 smaller balls, or mini 1-inch balls. Or use half the mixture for a medium-sized ball and the rest to make 8 to 10 mini balls.

To make mini pumpkin-shaped cheese balls

1. Shape the cheese mixture into 1-inch balls. Roll the balls in finely grated cheese to cover the outside.
2. Chill for 1 or more hours.
3. Use the side of a spoon handle to make about 5 indentations around each ball to form pumpkin grooves.
4. Just before serving, add pretzel sticks for stems and celery leaves for garnish.
5. Serve with crackers, pretzels, fresh veggie sticks, or grape clusters and apple slices.

FALL

Notes:

Makes 16 to 20 mini cheese balls

To make a large pumpkin-shaped cheese ball

1. Shape the cheese mixture into a large ball. Roll it in grated cheese to cover the outside. Wrap the ball in 2 layers of clear plastic wrap.
2. Place 3 or 4 rubber bands crisscrossed around the ball to form indentations like pumpkin grooves.
3. Chill for 2 hours.
4. Remove the bands and plastic wrap; add the pepper stem and celery leaf. (Or use a celery stick or large pretzel stick for the stem.)
5. Serve the cheese ball with crackers, pretzels, fresh veggie sticks, or grape clusters and apple slices.

Serves 16

Variations: *Bacon-Ranch Cheese Ball:* Add ⅓ cup crisp, crumbled bacon and 1 tablespoon dry ranch dressing mix to the cheese mixture. Mix well. Shape as desired.

Zesty Cheese Ball: Add ¼ cup chopped dried beef, 2 tablespoons finely chopped green onions, and ½ teaspoon dry mustard. Mix well. Shape as desired.

Fiesta Cheese Ball: Add ¼ cup salsa, drained, 1 tablespoon chopped cilantro, and a dash of chili powder if desired. Mix well. Shape as desired. Serve with tortilla chips.

Savory Cheese Ball: Add 1 teaspoon Worcestershire sauce, ¼ teaspoon garlic powder, and ¼ teaspoon onion powder to the cheese mixture. Mix well. Shape as desired.

Notes:

Sugar 'n' Spice Pecans

These are easy to make, and they are crunchy and sweet to eat or to share as a treat. *(From the kitchen of Great-Grandma Cheryl.)*

Difficulty:

Prep time: 10 minutes
Baking time: 70 minutes
Gluten-free

Gather with Grandma

5 cups pecan halves
1 egg white
1 tsp. water
½ tsp. vanilla
½ cup granulated sugar
½ tsp. cinnamon
¼ tsp. salt

Make with Grandma

1. Preheat the oven to 225°.
2. Select baking pan(s) with sides and cover them with parchment paper or lightly grease them. (Two 9 x 13-inch pans or one larger jelly roll pan work well.)
3. Place the pecans into a large bowl.
4. In a medium-sized mixing bowl, beat the egg white and water until the mixture is foamy. Stir in the vanilla.
5. Add the egg white mixture to the pecans. Stir until the pecans are well coated.
6. Combine the sugar, cinnamon, and salt. Sprinkle the mixture over the pecans and stir to thoroughly coat them.
7. Spread the pecans in a single layer on the prepared baking pan(s).
8. Bake the pecans for 70 minutes. Stir them every 20 minutes.
9. Leave the pecans on the baking sheet until they are completely cooled.
10. Store the pecans in an airtight container. Warning: They are so scrumptious, it is easy to just keep eating them by the handful after your first bite.

Makes 5 cups

Ideas: Make small nut cups for each place setting for Thanksgiving or a special dinner. Combine spiced pecans and a few fall candies of your choice.

Sugar 'n' Spice Pecans make wonderful gifts at Christmas or any time of year.

Notes:

Notes:

FALL

Teddy Bear Munch Mix

Perfect for a crunchy snack or a fun party treat.

Difficulty:

Prep time: 10 minutes

Gather with Grandma

- 1 cup bear-shaped graham crackers
- 1 cup honey-nut O-shaped cereal
- 1 cup square cereal, such as Chex (rice, corn, or wheat)
- 1 cup gummy bears
- ½ cup raisins
- ½ cup peanuts (optional)

Make with Grandma

1. Combine all the ingredients in a large bowl.
2. Mix them together with a large spoon.
3. Serve the mix in paper cups, bowls, or plastic bags. Munch away!

Makes 5 one-cup servings

A Spoonful of Sharing

Invite a cuddly teddy to join you as you nibble on this snack. You can enjoy it any day, but did you know September 9 is National Teddy Bear Day? Another September holiday is Grandparents Day, celebrated on the first Sunday after Labor Day. Grandparents Day is a time to honor grandparents and to give grandparents a chance to show love to their grandchildren. Proverbs 17:6 says, "Children's children [that means grandkids!] are a crown to the aged." It's a good day to hug your teddy and one another.

Notes:

Telescope Roll-Ups

You'll spy a tasty treat when you prepare these easy-to-make snacks. They taste like crisp cinnamon rolls.

Difficulty:

Prep time: 20 minutes
Bake time: 9 to 12 minutes

Gather with Grandma

8 slices white bread
½ cup whipped cream cheese
1 T. sugar
¼ tsp. vanilla
⅓ cup sugar
1 tsp. cinnamon
¼ cup (½ stick) butter, melted

Make with Grandma

1. Preheat the oven to 400°. Prepare a baking sheet with parchment paper.
2. Trim crusts from bread slices and roll slices flat with a rolling pin.
3. Mix together the cream cheese, 1 tablespoon sugar, and vanilla. Spread 1 tablespoon cheese mixture on each slice of bread. Roll each slice up tightly into a telescope.
4. Mix the remaining ⅓ cup sugar and cinnamon.
5. Brush each roll-up with melted butter and then roll it in the cinnamon-sugar mixture.
6. Arrange the telescopes on the prepared baking sheet with the seam side down. Bake for 9 to 12 minutes or until golden brown.
7. Serve them warm. They taste yummy with hot chocolate. Float a large marshmallow on the hot chocolate and pretend it's a planet you spied.

Makes 8 telescopes

Tip: Telescopes can be made ahead and frozen unbaked for up to 4 weeks. Bake them as needed for breakfast or a snack.

Notes:

Cornbread Pilgrim Hats

Big and little pilgrims will love these hats made from muffins. My grandsons thought the mini muffin hats looked the cutest.

Difficulty:

Prep time: 35 minutes

Gather with Grandma

1 (8.5 oz.) box cornbread mix
6-inch corn tortillas
Honey
Fruit leather (such as apple)
2 cheese slices for hat buckles

Make with Grandma

1. Preheat the oven according to the package directions.
2. Prepare the cornbread batter according to package directions. Spoon the batter into greased regular or mini muffin tins.
3. For mini muffins, bake them for 6 to 8 minutes or until browned and a toothpick comes out clean. For regular-sized muffins, bake them for 12 to 15 minutes or as the package suggests.
4. For small hats made from mini muffins, cut 2½-inch circles from tortillas to make the hat brims. For larger hats, cut 3-inch circles from the tortillas.
5. Cut off any rounded tops so the muffins lie flat. Spread honey on the muffin tops and then place each muffin upside down on a tortilla circle.
6. Using a pizza cutter and ruler, cut a ¼-inch-wide hatband from the fruit leather. With a toothpick, spread honey around the base of each muffin; attach a fruit leather band. If needed, hold the band in place with a piece of toothpick.
7. Cut a small square of cheese for a buckle and attach it to the band with honey.
8. Serve these pilgrim hats immediately with butter and honey.

Makes 8 large pilgrim hats or 18 small ones

Notes:

Easy Batter Bread

Soft center with crisp, crunchy crust. It smells so appetizing while baking that it's hard to wait to eat it. *(Inspired by a recipe from Oma Rosemarie in Indonesia.)*

Difficulty:

Prep time: 10 minutes to mix the batter
Rising time: 1½ hours
Baking time: 30 minutes

Gather with Grandma

1 cup warm water (115°)
2 tsp. yeast
1 T. sugar
2 cups all-purpose flour
1 tsp. salt
1 tsp. butter

Make with Grandma

1. Place the water in a small bowl, add the yeast and sugar, and stir to dissolve.
2. In a large bowl, combine the flour and salt.
3. Add the yeast mixture to the flour and stir it with a fork or wooden spoon until blended.
4. The mixture will be soft and sticky. Cover the bowl and let the batter rise for 1 hour in a warm place.
5. While the batter rises, grease a round 1-quart bowl with butter (or grease an 8-inch square pan or a large loaf pan).
6. When the mixture has risen to about double in size, stir it down with a spoon and transfer it into the greased bowl or baking pan.
7. Cover the batter and let it rise for another 30 minutes.
8. Preheat the oven to 425°.
9. Bake the bread for 15 minutes, and then reduce the oven temperature to 375° and bake it another 15 minutes. Remove the bread from the oven and tap the top with a wooden spoon. It's done when it sounds hollow. If it thuds, bake it for 5 more minutes.

Notes:

10. When done, remove the bread from the oven and place the pan on a cooling rack. After 5 minutes, loosen the sides of the bread with a table knife, remove from pan, and place the bread on a rack to cool.
11. Slice the bread and serve it warm with butter.

Serves 4 to 6

Tip: If you prefer a soft crust, place the cooled bread in a sealed bag or container.

Variations: *For whole wheat bread*: Substitute ½ cup whole wheat flour for white flour. You can also add up to ⅓ cup dried fruit, seeds, or nuts.

For raisin bread: Mix in ⅓ cup golden raisins. Sprinkle the top of the bread with a mixture of 1 teaspoon sugar and ¼ teaspoon cinnamon.

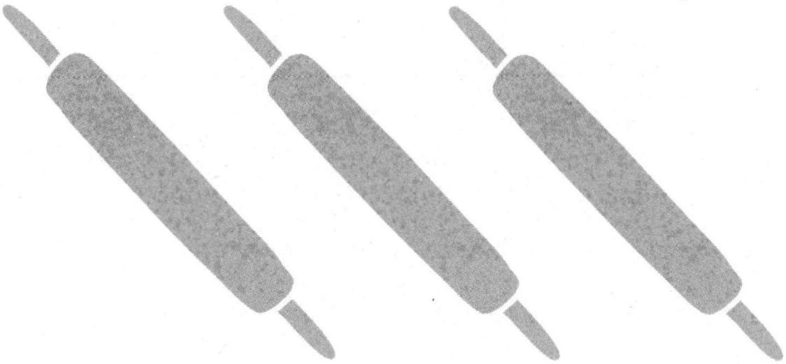

Notes:

Acorn Treats

These acorns are for people, not squirrels. They are easy to prepare and make cute party favors. After you finish making them, you can lick the chocolate frosting from your fingers.

Difficulty:

Prep time: 20 or 30 minutes, depending on how many you make

Gather with Grandma

24 mini Nilla Wafers
24 candy kisses, unwrapped
24 chocolate chips (regular or mini)
¼ cup chocolate frosting

Make with Grandma

1. Spread a dab of frosting on the flat side of the candy kiss and attach it in the center of the flat side of a vanilla wafer.
2. Add a dab of frosting to a chocolate chip and attach it on the rounded side of the wafer. That's it!
3. Now repeat these steps with the rest of the ingredients. Make 2 or 3 treats per person.

Makes 24 acorns

Notes:

Candy Corn Popcorn Cake

Sweeten someone's day with this chewy treat.

Difficulty:

Prep time: 30 minutes
Chilling time: 1 hour
Gluten-free option: Select gluten-free popcorn, candies, and nuts

Gather with Grandma

3½ quarts (14 cups) popped popcorn
½ cup (1 stick) butter, melted
1 (10 oz.) package miniature marshmallows
20 unwrapped caramels, cut in half
2 cups favorite small candies, such as candy corn, M&M's, gumdrops, or a mixture of candies
1 cup lightly salted or honey-roasted peanuts or mixed nuts (optional)

Make with Grandma

1. Lightly grease an angel food cake pan with butter or nonstick cooking spray.
2. Measure the popcorn into a large container that holds at least 5 quarts. Mix in the nuts and candy, except the chocolate candy. Measure the chocolate candy into a separate bowl to add later, otherwise the chocolate will melt and turn the cake brown.
3. In a large saucepan or microwave-safe bowl, melt the butter and caramels together until the caramels are soft, stirring with a wooden spoon. Add the marshmallows and melt them completely.
4. When melted, pour the marshmallow mixture over the popcorn mixture. Mix the cake with a wooden spoon.
5. After the mixture cools slightly, stir in the M&M's or other chocolate candy.
6. Press the popcorn mixture into the cake pan using wax paper or hands coated with butter. Press the mixture down until the cake is compact.
7. Refrigerate the cake for an hour or until firm.
8. Remove the cake from the pan and place it on a plate. Serve at room temperature. Use a serrated knife to slice the cake.

Notes:

9. To keep the cake fresh, wrap it tightly with plastic wrap or foil, or place it in an airtight container. This cake is best eaten in a few days. Wrap and refrigerate the uneaten cake to prevent it from becoming sticky.

Serves 12 to 16

Tip: For popcorn—use plain popcorn, kettle corn, or lightly salted and buttered popcorn. You can buy it already popped if you prefer. (A package of 5.5 ounces of popped popcorn will give you 14 cups.)

For candy, think seasonal variations:

- Fall: Add candy corn, pieces of orange candy slices or gumdrops, roasted pumpkin seeds, and peanuts.
- Christmas: Add red and green candies, such as M&M's and gumdrops. Or tint the cake green to look like a wreath. Decorate it with red candies or colorful sprinkles. Or cut green gumdrops into holly leaves. Add red-hot candies for holly berries.
- Valentine's Day: Tint the cake pink if you wish. Add your favorite red and white small candies and/or heart-shaped candies.

Ideas: Wrap the cake in foil, add a bow, and give away the whole cake. Or cut the cake into slices, package each slice in pretty cellophane or plastic bags, and give them as individual gifts. Or package several wrapped slices in an attractive tin.

Notes:

FALL

Frost on the Pumpkin Dessert

Pretend the whipped cream is frost on the pumpkin!

Difficulty:

Prep time: 30 minutes
Baking time: 45 to 50 minutes

Gather with Grandma

Crust

1 (15.25 oz.) package yellow cake mix, divided
½ cup (1 stick) butter, melted
1 egg

Filling

1 (30 oz.) large can pumpkin pie mix (not plain pumpkin)
⅔ cup milk
2 eggs

Topping

1 cup reserved dry cake mix
¼ cup softened butter
1 tsp. cinnamon
½ cup chopped walnuts or pecans (optional)
Whipped cream
Candy corn for garnish

See page 38 for Homemade Whipped Cream.

Make with Grandma

1. Preheat the oven to 350°.
2. Empty the cake mix into a large mixing bowl. Remove 1 cup of the dry cake mix and set it aside.
3. Add the melted butter and the egg to the cake mix in the large bowl. Mix the ingredients until they are well blended.
4. Spray the bottom of a 9 x 13-inch baking pan with nonstick cooking spray. Press the crust mixture into the pan.

Notes:

5. In the large bowl, beat together the pumpkin pie mix, milk, and eggs. Pour this mixture over the crust.
6. For the topping, combine the 1 cup reserved cake mix with butter, cinnamon, and nuts. Drop this mixture by small spoonfuls over the pumpkin filling.
7. Bake the dessert for 45 to 50 minutes or until a knife inserted into the center comes out clean.
8. Cool slightly. Refrigerate the dessert until it is firm.
9. Use a round cookie cutter or drinking glass to cut the dessert into circles. Cut the circles close together and save the dessert between them to eat later.
10. Place each "pumpkin" on a dessert plate. Add a spoonful of whipped cream and a candy corn "stem." Refrigerate unused portions. This dessert also freezes well.

Makes 12 pumpkins

Shortcut: Cut the dessert into squares. Add a dollop of whipped cream and a candy corn.

A Spoonful of Sharing

With Thanksgiving coming soon, my daughter Anita asked her preschool-aged son, "Are you thankful?"

"No," he replied. "I'm Peter."

He's a young adult now, and yes, he *is* thankful.

Thankful is a word "full of thanks." Who can you thank? Is it ever hard to be thankful?

"Give thanks to the LORD, for he is good! His faithful love endures forever" (Psalm 106:1 NLT).

Notes:

Handmade Fruit Pie

Any way you slice it, making this pie together will be fun. Each of you can trace one hand onto paper to use as a pattern for the upper crust. After the pie is baked, give yourselves a hand as you eat a warm slice topped with vanilla ice cream.

Difficulty:

Prep time: 45 minutes to make
Baking time: 30 to 35 minutes
Gluten-free option: Use gluten-free piecrusts

Gather with Grandma

2 unbaked piecrusts, ready-made or homemade
2 (21 oz.) cans prepared pie filling (apple, cherry, blueberry, or favorite filling)
Sheets of paper for making hand patterns
Powdered sugar (optional)
Ice cream (optional)

For homemade piecrust, see page 156 for the recipe I use with Cascade Blackberry Pie.

Make with Grandma

1. Preheat the oven to 425°.
2. Unroll 1 piecrust and place it in a 9-inch pie pan. Flute the edge of the crust with your fingers or press the edge of the crust lightly with a fork to make a design.
3. Fill the crust with your favorite prepared fruit filling.
4. Trace 1 grandparent's hand and 1 grandchild's hand on paper. Cut out the hand patterns.
5. For the top crust, lay the second piecrust flat on a lightly floured surface. Place the hand patterns on the crust and cut out the shapes with a table knife.
6. Overlap the hands on top of the fruit for the top crust. Now you're part of the upper crust!
7. Place the pie on a cookie sheet in case the filling bubbles over. Bake the pie

Notes:

for 20 minutes and then reduce the oven temperature to 375° so it won't get too brown.

8. Bake the pie an additional 15 to 20 minutes until the crust is golden brown. If the edge of the crust begins to brown too much, cover it with aluminum foil.
9. Cool the pie on a rack. If desired, dust the hand-shaped crust with powdered sugar.
10. When the pie is cool, serve it à la mode with vanilla ice cream.

Serves 6 to 8

Variations: For cherry filling, add ¼ teaspoon almond flavoring to the fruit filling. For apple, add 1 teaspoon cinnamon and ½ teaspoon nutmeg to the fruit filling.

A Spoonful of Sharing

Perhaps you'll use this recipe to make apple pie. The Bible says we are the apple of God's eye, which means we are very precious to Him. Here's an Apple of His Eye Pie recipe with a different list of ingredients (adapted from Grandma Rae's recipe).

Apple of His Eye Pie
Apples: Psalm 17:8
Sugar: Psalm 119:103
Spices: 2 Corinthians 2:14
Folds of Crust: Ephesians 4:16 AMPC

What would these ingredients yield in our lives?

FALL

Winter

Holiday thrills, winter chills, and time to sit by a cozy fire. 'Tis the season to share love and make memories as you build snowmen and sip hot chocolate with candy cane stirrers. With grandkids on break from school, there's more time to celebrate traditions and special holidays. Christmas, New Year's Day, and Valentine's Day make the perfect times to stir up winter fun in the kitchen.

As long as the earth endures, seedtime and harvest, cold and heat, summer and winter, day and night will never cease.

GENESIS 8:22

Winter

Notes:

Sausage Triangles

These flavorful sausage triangles look impressive made with puff pastry that browns beautifully. My daughter-in-law, Amy, introduced me to this yummy recipe, which is one of their family favorites.

Difficulty: 🥄🥄🥄

Prep time: 45 minutes
Baking time: 15 to 20 minutes for each baking sheet

Gather with Grandma

3 T. oil for frying
¾ lb. ground Italian sausage or sweet Italian sausage (remove casings if you use links)
3 cups hash brown potatoes, thawed (Southern-style, diced)
⅓ cup onion, finely chopped (or 1 or 2 T. minced dry onion)
1 tsp. dried thyme (optional, but it adds a lot of flavor)
2 sheets frozen puff pastry, thawed
1 large egg, lightly beaten

Make with Grandma

1. Preheat the oven to 425°. Prepare the baking sheets with nonstick cooking spray or parchment paper.
2. Heat the oil in a large skillet on medium heat. Add the sausage, breaking it up, and potatoes, onion, and thyme.
3. Fry and stir the mixture until the sausage is browned and the potatoes are cooked, about 10 to 15 minutes.
4. Place 1 sheet of pastry onto a lightly floured surface. With a rolling pin, roll the sheet into a 12-inch square. Using a pizza cutter, cut the sheet into 3 4-inch-wide strips. Then cut each strip into three 4-inch squares.
5. Place 1 or 2 heaping spoonfuls of meat filling in the center of each square.
6. Fold the pastry over diagonally from point to point to form a triangle. Seal the edges. Place the triangles on the prepared baking sheet.
7. Repeat with the other sheet of pastry. Each sheet makes 9 triangles.
8. Brush the triangles lightly with the beaten egg.

Notes:

9. Bake for 15 to 20 minutes or until the triangles are puffed and brown.
10. Carefully remove the baking sheet from the oven. Remove the triangles to a cooling rack.
11. Serve the triangles warm with mustard or Zippy Dip (see page 59) if desired.

Makes 18 triangles

Notes:

Savory Holiday Meatballs

Always a festive favorite in our home, these meatballs are easy to serve in a Crock-Pot at a holiday buffet. But they taste wonderful any time of year. (*Inspired by a recipe from Grandma MaryAnn.*)

Difficulty:

Prep time: 30 minutes
Baking time: 30 minutes
Gluten-free option: Use gluten-free Worcestershire sauce

Gather with Grandma

Meatballs

2 lbs. lean ground beef
2 eggs, beaten
½ cup quick oatmeal
2 T. minced dried onion
1 T. Worcestershire sauce
1 tsp. salt
¼ tsp. garlic powder
Dash of pepper

Sauce

1 (14 oz.) can jellied cranberry sauce
1 (12 oz.) bottle chili sauce
4 tsp. brown sugar
2 tsp. lemon juice

Make with Grandma

1. Preheat the oven to 350°.
2. In a large bowl, combine the ground beef, eggs, and oatmeal. Mix well.
3. In a small container combine all the rest of the meatball ingredients, and add them to the beef mixture. Mix thoroughly.
4. Shape the meat mixture into 1-inch meatballs.
5. Place the meatballs in a baking pan with sides. Bake for 25 to 30 minutes or until no longer pink inside.

Notes:

6. While the meatballs bake, combine the sauce ingredients in a large saucepan. Heat on medium and stir the sauce ingredients to blend. Turn off until the meatballs are done.
7. When the meatballs are baked, cool them for a few minutes. Then remove them with a slotted spoon, leaving the grease in the pan. Add the meatballs to the sauce. Simmer for 5 to 10 minutes until the meatballs are glazed.
8. If serving them at a buffet, serve the meatballs from a Crock-Pot with toothpicks to poke into them. Or you can serve them over cooked rice.

Makes about 60 small meatballs

Shortcut: Buy prepared meatballs. Add them to the sauce, heat, and eat!

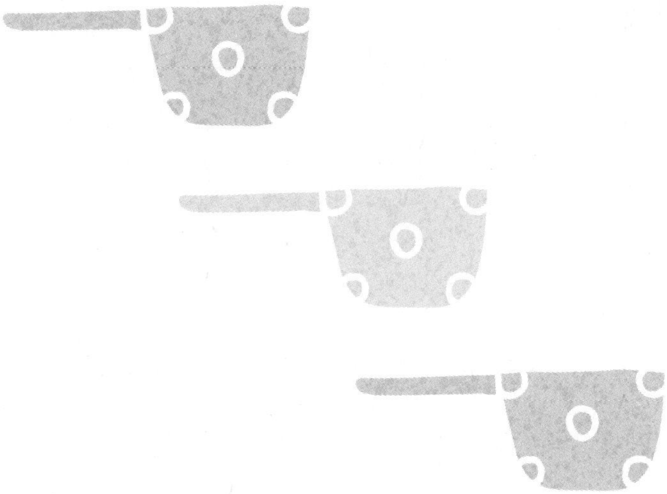

Notes:

Smiley Joes

You'll smile when you eat this satisfying sandwich in a bun.

Difficulty: 🥄🥄🥄

Prep time: 40 minutes
Gluten-free option: Use gluten-free buns and Worcestershire sauce

Gather with Grandma

Meat Filling

1 lb. lean ground beef
¼ cup minced celery
1 T. minced dried onion (or ⅓ cup chopped fresh onion)
1 (15 oz.) can tomato sauce
¼ cup ketchup
1 T. brown sugar, firmly packed
1 T. Worcestershire sauce
1 T. vinegar
½ tsp. dry mustard powder
¼ tsp. salt
Dash of pepper
Garnishes to make a face: stuffed green or black olives, pickles, red pepper, and grated cheese. Carrot and celery sticks for arms and legs

Buns

6 sliced hamburger buns
3 T. butter (optional)

Make with Grandma

1. Preheat the oven to 325°.
2. Brown the ground beef, celery, and onion in a skillet. Carefully pour off the grease.
3. Stir in the remaining filling ingredients and cover the skillet with a lid.
4. Simmer the meat mixture over low heat for about 15 minutes, stirring occasionally. Watch carefully so the mixture doesn't burn on the bottom. Add 2 tablespoons of water to the meat mixture if it becomes too thick.

Notes:

5. While the meat simmers, lightly butter the hamburger buns. Wrap them in aluminum foil and warm them in the oven for 5 to 10 minutes.
6. When the meat mixture is ready, spoon it onto a bottom bun and close it with the top bun.
7. Each person can decorate the top bun with olive slices for eyes, a pickle circle for a nose, a slice of red pepper for a smile, and grated cheese for hair. Or you could make the smiley face on the meat mixture and then add the top bun.
8. Serve your Smiley Joes with carrot and celery sticks. Use them to make a stick figure with arms and legs below the bun head. For once, you get to play with your food!

Makes 6 servings

Shortcut: Brown the meat, add 1 (16 oz.) can purchased sloppy joe sauce or use a packet of dry sloppy joe mix. Prepare the mix according to the package directions. Fill the buns with the hot meat mixture. Decorate each top bun to make a smiley face.

A Spoonful of Sharing

As you create foods together in the kitchen, chat about where your desire to create comes from. Are we creative because we are made in the image of our Creator God? Perhaps you could memorize and talk about this verse together. "Remember your Creator in the days of your youth" (Ecclesiastes 12:1).

Notes:

Tasty Toboggans

Our family's tradition is to make sleds for breakfast when it snows. These French toast toboggans will slide right into your mouth on their bacon runners!

Difficulty:

Prep time: 10 minutes to make 3 toboggans
Gluten-free Option: Use gluten-free bread and gluten-free bacon or sausage

Gather with Grandma

3 slices bread
1 egg
¼ cup milk
½ tsp. vanilla
¼ tsp. cinnamon (optional)
6 slices bacon or link sausages
Powdered sugar
Butter, syrup, honey, and/or jam

Make with Grandma

1. Beat the egg and stir in the milk, vanilla, and cinnamon if desired.
2. Heat a griddle or skillet to medium high and spray it with nonstick cooking spray.
3. Dip each slice of bread into the egg mixture. Cook the slices until the French toast is golden brown on each side.
4. Place the bacon slices on paper towels on a microwave-safe container or on a plate. Cover the bacon with another paper towel to prevent splattering.
5. Microwave the bacon until crisp (2 to 4 minutes).
6. Carefully remove the bacon. It will be hot.
7. Place 2 slices of bacon on a plate for runners.
8. Top the runners with 1 piece of French toast for the toboggan.
9. Sprinkle with sifted powdered sugar "snow."
10. Serve with butter, syrup, honey, and jam.

Makes 3 toboggans

Notes:

A Spoonful of Sharing

My grandkids consider snow a magical part of winter. Whether you have snow or not, chat about snow while you eat these toboggans. When was the last time you enjoyed snow? What did you do in the snow? The Bible mentions snow in Isaiah 1:18 and Psalm 51:7, which says, "Wash me, and I shall be whiter than snow." Can you think of anything whiter than snow? These verses remind us that no matter what we say or do, God can cleanse and make us new.

Notes:

Crisp Veggie Wreath

Festive and healthy to munch! A colorful wreath served with your favorite dip.

Difficulty:

Prep time: 10 minutes
Gluten-free

Gather with Grandma

3 cups raw broccoli pieces
3 cups raw cauliflower pieces
1 to 2 cups cherry or grape tomatoes
Favorite vegetable dip
1 red or green bell pepper
12-inch round plate or pizza pan

Make with Grandma

1. Wash the fresh vegetables and let them dry on a paper towel.
2. Cut the top off the pepper and remove the seeds. Place the empty pepper in the center of the platter to hold the dip for the veggies.
3. Break the broccoli and cauliflower into bite-sized pieces.
4. Arrange mounds of broccoli, cauliflower, and tomatoes around the pepper. Alternate bunches of green, white, and red vegetables about 3 or 4 times until the platter is full and you have created a colorful wreath. Cover the wreath with plastic wrap and refrigerate it until ready to serve.
5. To serve, fill the pepper with dip, such as homemade Ranch Dressing and Dip (page 148). Refrigerate the leftovers.

Serves 8 to 10

Variation: Make the wreath with any combination of green, white, and red vegetables of your choice, such as cucumber slices, snap peas, green beans, jicama, radishes, and red pepper.

Notes:

Fresh Strawberry Hearts and Dip

This is my granddaughter Anna's favorite way to eat fresh strawberries. To her, the berries taste like they are dipped in caramel sauce.

Difficulty: 

Prep time: 10 minutes
Gluten-free

Gather with Grandma

Fresh whole strawberries (use ones that have pointed ends)
Sour cream
Brown sugar

Make with Grandma

1. Wash the strawberries and remove the stems. Anna removes them by poking a plastic straw from the point of the strawberry up to the stem. The straw makes the stem pop off.
2. To make heart-shaped strawberries, use a plastic knife and cut a "V" shape on the top of the berry. If you don't remove the stem with a straw, you can also remove the stem as you cut a "V" shape in the strawberry.
3. Spoon sour cream and brown sugar into separate small bowls.
4. Everyone helps themselves to the berries, brown sugar, and sour cream. To eat the strawberries, first dip them into sour cream and then into brown sugar. Take a bite and you'll say, "Mmm, yummy!" You'll want more than 1 strawberry.

Prepare as many as needed

Ideas: Serve strawberries with melted chocolate, sprinkles, chopped nuts, coconut, mini chocolate chips, or whipped cream. Dip the berries into melted chocolate and then the toppings you like.

Tip: Cut whole heart-shaped strawberries into vertical slices to make heart slices. Serve them as fruit topping on pancakes or strawberry shortcake.

Edible Igloos

A cool idea that will make you shiver with delight. At age seven, my grandson Alex made this igloo by himself.

Difficulty: 

Prep Time: 20 minutes
Gluten-free

Gather with Grandma

Apples (one half per person)
Creamy peanut butter
Miniature marshmallows

Make with Grandma

1. Cut an apple in half vertically from the stem down. Remove the apple core.
2. Set one-half apple, cut side down, on a plate or a piece of wax paper.
3. With a table knife, spread a thin layer of peanut butter on the outside peel of the apple.
4. Place marshmallows in a circle around the base of the apple. Leave a small space for the igloo's "door." Continue to add rows of marshmallows, moving up as you finish each row. Enjoy your delightful creation!

1 apple makes 2 igloos

Notes:

Notes:

Great Grins

You'll be all smiles when you make this fun treat!

Difficulty:

Prep time: 20 minutes
Gluten-free

Gather with Grandma

1 red apple
Whipped cream cheese
White miniature marshmallows

Make with Grandma

1. Cut the apple into quarters, remove the core, and cut each quarter into ½-inch-thick slices. These slices become the lips.
2. Spread a thin layer of cream cheese on 1 side of an apple slice.
3. Face the red apple peel toward you to make the lower lip. Stick 5 to 8 marshmallows (flat ends down) on top of the cream cheese for teeth.
4. Spread cream cheese on another apple slice and place the slice (peel facing toward you) on top of the marshmallows. Press down gently. There's your great grin!
5. Make more smiles.

Each apple makes 5 or 6 grins

Variation: For Nutty Grins, use peanut butter instead of cream cheese to hold the apple slices and marshmallows together. Spread the peanut butter toward the back of the apple slice so it doesn't discolor the marshmallow teeth.

A Spoonful of Sharing

Proverbs 15:13 (MSG) says, "A cheerful heart brings a smile to your face." What makes you smile? What makes God smile? How can we bring joy to someone?

WINTER

Notes:

Midnight Munchies

You won't want to wait until midnight on New Year's Eve to munch on this snack. The bugles remind us to listen for the trumpet, which will sound for Christ's return.

Difficulty: 🥄🥄

Prep time: 15 minutes
Baking time: 1 hour

Gather with Grandma

3 cups wheat cereal squares
3 cups rice cereal squares
3 cups original Bugles
2 cups pretzel sticks, broken in half
1 cup peanuts or mixed nuts (optional)
6 T. butter
1 tsp. Worcestershire sauce
½ tsp. garlic powder

Make with Grandma

1. Heat the oven to 250°.
2. In a large bowl, mix together the cereals, Bugles, pretzels, and nuts.
3. In a small microwave-safe bowl, melt the butter and stir in seasonings.
4. Pour the butter mixture over the cereal mixture and stir until evenly coated.
5. Divide the mixture into two 9 x 13-inch baking pans. Bake for 1 hour, stirring every 15 minutes.
6. Spread the snack on paper towels to cool. Store in an airtight container.

Makes 12 cups

Notes:

A Spoonful of Sharing

As you munch on this snack with Bugles, talk about the exciting time ahead when the trumpet will sound for Christ's return. "It will happen in a moment, in the blink of an eye, when the last trumpet is blown. For when the trumpet sounds, those who have died will be raised to live forever. And we who are living will also be transformed" (1 Corinthians 15:52 NLT). Come soon, Lord Jesus!

Notes:

Funtastic New Year's Pretzels

Ring in the New Year with these yummy, soft pretzels. Or have fun making them together any time of the year.

Difficulty:

Prep time: 30 minutes hands-on
Rising time: 1 hour
Baking time: 12 minutes for each baking sheet

Gather with Grandma

1½ cups warm milk (115°)
1 T. yeast
3 T. brown sugar
2 T. butter, melted
1½ tsp. salt
3½ cups white flour
½ cup whole wheat flour
1 egg, slightly beaten (to brush on pretzels before baking)
Coarse salt, sesame seeds, or poppy seeds
1 T. sugar
1 tsp. cinnamon
Dipping sauces of your choice

Make with Grandma

1. In a medium-sized bowl, combine the warm milk, yeast, and brown sugar. Stir to dissolve. Wait a few minutes for the yeast to start working, and then stir in the butter and salt.
2. In a large bowl, combine the flours. Add the wet ingredients to the flour and stir until blended.
3. On a lightly floured surface, knead the dough for 1 or 2 minutes until it's smooth and elastic.
4. Place the dough in a bowl and cover it with buttered foil so the bread won't stick to the foil when it rises. Set the dough in a warm place for 1 hour or until the dough doubles in size.
5. Preheat the oven to 425°. Lightly spray the cookie sheets with nonstick cooking spray.

Notes:

6. Roll pieces of dough into finger-thick strips. Shape them into letters, numbers, or whatever shapes you like. For the New Year, make numbers for the year—for example 2020. Or shape letters for words or initials for names. Place them on the baking sheets.
7. Brush the pretzels with the beaten egg. Mix the cinnamon and sugar. Sprinkle the pretzels with coarse salt, seeds, or with the cinnamon-and-sugar mixture.
8. Bake the pretzels for 10 to 12 minutes, or until golden brown. Cool them slightly on a wire rack.
9. Serve the warm pretzels plain or with dipping sauces such as mustard, honey mustard, melted butter, cream cheese, or grated cheese.

Makes about 20 shapes, depending on their size

Ideas: You could make the dough ahead and have it ready to shape with your grandchild. It would also be fun to make these pretzels for a birthday party with your grandchild's new age in numbers.

A Spoonful of Sharing

What are you looking forward to this year? If you could plan the year, what would you write on the calendar? According to Jeremiah 29:11, God already has plans for us. What kind of plans does this verse say He has? "'For I know the plans I have for you,' declares the Lord, 'plans to prosper you and not to harm you, plans to give you hope and a future.'" God knows everything that will happen to us this year, and He will take care of us.

WINTER

Notes:

Puffy Pancake

Four simple ingredients add up to a delightful breakfast popular with my grandkids. The pancake puffs up like a popover.

Difficulty:

Prep time: 10 minutes
Baking time: 15 to 20 minutes

Gather with Grandma

3 T. butter
3 eggs
¾ cup flour
¾ cup milk
Toppings, such as powdered sugar, syrup, honey, jam, whipped cream, and fruit

Make with Grandma

1. Preheat the oven to 425°.
2. Place the butter in an ovenproof dish or baking pan (e.g., large cast-iron frying pan, deep-dish glass pie pan, or an 8-inch square cake pan). Place the pan with butter in the oven for a few minutes to melt the butter. Watch carefully so the butter doesn't burn.
3. Carefully remove the pan from the oven and spread the melted butter evenly in the pan.
4. Crack the eggs into a medium-sized mixing bowl and beat them until mixed and light yellow.
5. Add the flour and milk. Beat the mixture together until no lumps remain.
6. Pour the batter into the baking pan. Bake the mixture for 15 to 20 minutes until the pancake is puffed and golden brown.
7. When the puffy pancake comes out of the oven, it's quite a showstopper. Serve it immediately because it will flatten quickly. Don't be alarmed.
8. Enjoy this yummy treat with toppings of your choice. (See page 38 for Homemade Whipped Cream.)

Serves 2 to 4 or 1 very hungry grandchild!

Notes:

Floating Frosty Snowmen

These snowmen are fun to serve floating in a mug of hot chocolate.

Difficulty: 

Prep time: 10 minutes

Gather with Grandma

1 cup whipped cream or frozen whipped topping
¼ cup mini chocolate chips
Orange gumdrop

Make with Grandma

1. Drop 1 tablespoon portions of whipped cream or topping onto a wax paper-lined pan. These should be small enough to float in a mug. Shape them into snowballs to make a snowman's head.
2. Add 2 chips for eyes and 3 or 4 chips for the mouth.
3. For the nose, use a small piece of an orange gumdrop.
4. Freeze the snowballs until you are ready to enjoy a cup of hot chocolate. (See Snowman's Delight Hot Chocolate recipe on page 127.) Float a Frosty Snowman on top of the hot chocolate. Make the hot chocolate extra hot because the frozen snowman will cool it.

Makes about 12 snowmen

Notes:

Snowman's Delight Hot Chocolate

A comforting winter warm-up for a snowy day or any day. Pretend the marshmallows are snowballs melting in the steaming drink.

Difficulty: 

Prep time: 10 minutes
Gluten-free option: Make sure the cocoa mix, creamer, and all toppings are gluten-free (Swiss Miss is gluten-free.)

Gather with Grandma

2 cups instant nonfat dry milk
1 cup sweetened hot cocoa mix
½ cup powdered sugar, sifted
½ cup unsweetened cocoa powder
¼ cup vanilla powder nondairy creamer
⅛ tsp. salt
Whipped cream, mini marshmallows, candy canes, and sprinkles (optional)

Make with Grandma

1. In a large bowl, mix together all the dry ingredients with a wire whisk.
2. Store the mix in a covered jar or container.
3. To serve, heat 1 cup milk (or water) per person. Stir in ¼ cup hot chocolate mix. Add more if you prefer it stronger. Top with marshmallows or whipped cream. My grandkids like marshmallows and whipped cream with sprinkles on top. Or serve with Floating Frosty Snowmen (page 126). The hot chocolate is also tasty with a sprinkle of cinnamon or a candy cane for stirring.

Makes about 4 cups hot chocolate mix

WINTER

Notes:

Banana-Split Bowls

Scoop up a scrumptious sundae with bananas and your favorite toppings. Everyone can make this dessert to suit his or her taste.

Difficulty:

Prep Time: 15 minutes
Gluten-free option: Use gluten-free cookies, wafers, and toppings

Gather with Grandma

Bananas, peeled and split in half lengthwise
Vanilla or Neapolitan ice cream
Strawberries, sliced
Crushed pineapple, drained
Chocolate syrup
Whipped cream
Chopped nuts (optional)
Sprinkles
Maraschino cherries
Chocolate cookies such as Oreos
Vanilla wafers

Make with Grandma

1. Fill serving bowls with fruit and toppings and place them on the serving table. Individuals make their own banana splits by adding the fruits and toppings they like.
2. Place a split banana in a bowl. Add 1 to 3 scoops of ice cream down the middle between the banana halves.
3. Add toppings in the order listed in the recipe, ending with a cherry on top.
4. If desired, crumble cookies or wafers on top, or eat them with the banana split.

Make 1 for each person (and maybe some will want seconds)

Notes:

Cranberry Shortcake with Butter-Rum Sauce

A tasty treat, especially during the holidays. The sweet butter-rum sauce complements the tart cranberries in the shortcake. *(From the kitchen of Grandma Ruth, my sister.)*

Difficulty:

Prep time for shortcake: 25 minutes
Prep time for sauce: 10 minutes
Baking time: 25 to 30 minutes
Gluten-free: Sauce only

Gather with Grandma

Shortcake

3 cups flour
1 cup sugar
1 T. baking powder
¾ tsp. salt
1½ cups milk
½ cup shortening, melted
1 tsp. vanilla
2 cups fresh cranberries (or frozen cranberries, thawed)

Sauce

½ cup (1 stick) butter, melted
1 cup sugar
½ cup cream
1 tsp. rum extract (or use vanilla, lemon, orange, or almond)

Make with Grandma

1. Preheat the oven to 350°. Grease a 9 x 13-inch baking pan.
2. Mix together the flour, sugar, baking powder, and salt.
3. Stir in the milk, shortening, and vanilla.
4. Fold in the cranberries.
5. Spoon the thick batter into the prepared pan. Bake the cake for 25 to 30

Notes:

minutes or until a toothpick inserted into the middle comes out clean. While the shortcake bakes, make the sauce.

6. Place the shortcake on a cooling rack until serving time. (It's best served while still warm.)
7. For the sauce, combine the butter, sugar, and cream in a saucepan. Cook over medium heat and stir with a wooden spoon until the mixture comes to a boil.
8. Remove the sauce from the heat and stir in the rum extract or the flavoring of your choice.
9. Pour the warm sauce over individual servings of warm shortcake. Refrigerate the leftover sauce in a covered container. It keeps for 2 weeks.

Serves 12 to 15

Variation: Replace the cranberries with other berries, such as blueberries. The sauce makes a rich topping for ice cream and other desserts. You can substitute other flavorings.

Double-Thumbprint Heart Cookies

These buttery shortbread cookies, filled with jam, make a special treat for Valentine's Day or any day. Start with two small cookie balls side-by-side. Then grandma and grandchild can add a thumbprint—one on each ball. Next, shape the balls to form a heart, joining the thumbprints in each cookie.

Difficulty:

Prep time: 45 to 60 minutes
Baking time: 12 to 15 minutes per baking sheet

Gather with Grandma

Cookies

1 cup (2 sticks) butter, softened
⅔ cup sugar
1 tsp. almond extract (or vanilla extract)
2 cups flour
Pink food coloring
½ cup seedless raspberry jam

Glaze

1 cup powdered sugar
1 tsp. almond extract (or vanilla extract)
2 to 3 tsp. water

Make with Grandma

1. Preheat the oven to 350°.
2. In a large bowl, cream together the butter, sugar, and almond extract.
3. Add the flour gradually and mix the ingredients together by hand.
4. Knead the dough on a lightly floured surface until it is blended and smooth.
5. Divide the dough in half. If desired, tint one-half light pink.
6. Shape the dough into ½-inch balls (slightly larger than a marble).
7. On an ungreased baking sheet, place 2 cookies side by side so they touch. If you made half the dough pink, place 1 pink and 1 white ball side by side. Or make some cookies with 2 white balls or 2 pink balls.

Notes:

Notes:

8. Make a hole in the center of each cookie ball with your finger or thumb. Grandma and grandchild can each make a thumbprint in one of the balls.
9. Shape the lower part of the cookie to a point to form a heart. Flatten the dough between the holes to join the thumbprints and make one larger hole.
10. Fill the center of each heart with ¼ to ½ teaspoon jam.
11. Bake the cookies for 12 to 15 minutes or until they are firm but not brown.
12. Remove the cookies from the oven. Cool the cookies for about 10 minutes before adding glaze if desired.
13. Mix together the powdered sugar, almond extract, and water. Drizzle the glaze over the cookies with a fork.
14. When the glaze is firm and the cookies are cool, place the hearts in a covered container.

Makes 3 dozen cookies

A Spoonful of Sharing

If you could write words on conversation heart candies, what would you say? If God wrote the words on candy hearts, what would He say to us? Draw several hearts and write a short message on each. Look for ideas in Psalm 103:11 and 1 John 4:19. In 1 John 3:1 it says, "See what great love the Father has lavished on us, that we should be called children of God! And that is what we are!"

Notes:

Frosted Nativity Cookies

Cutout cookies at Christmas have been a meaningful tradition in our family for decades. Making, baking, and frosting cookies takes time, so you'll have lots of finger-lickin' fun. With young grandkids, prepare the dough beforehand. Or bake the cookies ahead and just frost and decorate them with your grandkids. During other seasons of the year, cut the cookies into different shapes.

Difficulty:

Prep time: Allow several hours to enjoy this activity
Baking time: 7 or 8 minutes for each cookie sheet

Gather with Grandma

Cookie dough

1 cup (2 sticks) butter, softened
1½ cups powdered sugar, sifted
1 egg
1 tsp. vanilla
½ tsp. almond flavoring (optional)
2¾ cups flour
1 tsp. baking soda
1 tsp. cream of tartar
½ tsp. salt

Frosting

2 cups powdered sugar, sifted
¼ cup (½ stick) butter, softened
2 T. milk (add 1 more tablespoon at a time if needed)
1 tsp. vanilla flavoring
Food coloring
Sprinkles

Make with Grandma

1. In a large bowl, cream together the butter and sugar. Mix in the egg and flavorings.
2. In a medium-sized bowl, combine the flour, baking soda, cream of tartar, and salt.
3. Add the dry ingredients to the creamed mixture and mix well.

Notes:

4. Divide the cookie dough in half and form it into 2 flat circles.
5. Wrap the dough and refrigerate it for 1 or 2 hours or until it is easy to handle.
6. Preheat the oven to 375°. Spray cookie sheets with nonstick cooking spray.
7. On a lightly floured surface, roll the dough about ¼ inch thick. Cut the dough with cookie cutter shapes of your choice. For Christmas, use angels, stars, and other Nativity shapes.
8. Place the cookies on the prepared cookie sheets. Bake the cutouts for 7 or 8 minutes or until light golden brown around the edges.
9. Remove the baking sheet and place it on a cooling rack. When partially cooled, remove the cookies from the baking sheet.
10. To make the frosting, mix together the powdered sugar, butter, milk, and vanilla until smooth and creamy. Add food coloring if desired.
11. Frost and decorate the cookies when completely cool.

Makes about 5 dozen 2- to 2½-inch cookies

Tip: Select cookie cutters according to the holiday or season.

- Christmas: Nativity-shaped cutters. Order online if you can't find them in stores.
- Valentine's Day: Heart-shaped cookies. Cut the dough into hearts. With a small cookie cutter, cut out centers of half the hearts before baking. After they are baked and cooled, spread a little raspberry jam on the whole cookies. Top them with a cookie with the center cut out. The red jam shows through. Sprinkle with powdered sugar if desired.
- Fall: Leaves, apples, pumpkins, and crescent moon cookies create fun.

A Spoonful of Sharing

While you enjoy cookies and milk, read the Christmas story from the Bible (Luke 2:1-20) or a children's book. Or listen to a recorded version. The grandkids could also use the Nativity-shaped cookies to tell the story of Jesus's birth. Then fill colorful tins with cookies to send home with your grandchildren.

Notes:

Peppermint Angel Cake

Our family often celebrates Jesus's birthday with a birthday cake and candles. This angel food cake with whipped cream and crushed peppermint candy seems just right for His birthday. But it tastes scrumptious all year. During other seasons, replace the peppermint candy with fresh strawberries or favorite toppings. *(Inspired by Grandma Myrtle's recipe.)*

Difficulty:

Prep time: 20 minutes

Gather with Grandma

1 angel food cake, store-bought or homemade
1½ cups heavy whipping cream
3 T. granulated sugar
3 T. powdered sugar
1 tsp. vanilla
¾ cup peppermint candy, crushed
Small candy canes (1 per person)
Birthday candles
Ice cream (optional)

Make with Grandma

1. Cut the prepared cake in half horizontally. Use a serrated knife and cut with sawing motions. Place the cake on a serving plate.
2. Whip the cream with an electric mixer until soft peaks form. Mix in the sugars and vanilla.
3. Spread whipped cream on the bottom layer. If desired, sprinkle 2 tablespoons crushed peppermint candy on top of the whipped cream. Add the top half of the cake.
4. Frost the rest of the cake with whipped cream. Frost the sides first. Finish with the top. If you have whipped cream left, save it to serve with the cake. Refrigerate the cake until ready to serve.
5. Just before serving, sprinkle crushed peppermint candy on top of the cake and also on the sides if desired. If you add the candy more than a half hour before serving, the peppermint will begin to run.

Notes:

6. To get the candy to stick on the sides, toss it gently from an inch away.
7. Add candy canes and candles on top. Light the candles and sing "Happy Birthday" to Jesus.
8. Cut the cake with a serrated knife. Serve with ice cream if desired.

Serves 8 to 10

A Spoonful of Sharing

Candy canes are popular at Christmas and can remind us of Jesus. As you eat your cake and nibble your candy canes, read this poem, and talk about how candy canes point to Jesus.

The Candy Cane
Author Unknown

Look at the candy cane
What do you see?
Stripes that are red
Like the blood shed for me.

White is for my Savior
Who's sinless and pure.
"J" is for Jesus my Lord,
that's for sure!

Turn it around
And a staff you will see.
Jesus my shepherd
Was born just for me!

Happy birthday, Jesus! We love You. You're the best present at Christmas.

Notes:

Soda Cracker Toffee

Sweet confections lead to sweet connections. This candy, which tastes like Almond Roca, makes a great gift. No one will guess it's made with saltine crackers. *(A favorite of Grandma Pam.)*

Difficulty:

Prep and bake time: 30 minutes

Gather with Grandma

50 saltine crackers (about 2 sleeves)
1 cup (2 sticks) butter
1 cup brown sugar, firmly packed
1 (12 oz.) pkg. dark chocolate chips (2 cups)
½ cup almonds, sliced or slivered

Make with Grandma

1. Preheat the oven to 350°.
2. Butter an 11 x 18-inch jelly roll pan with butter or line it with parchment paper.
3. Place a single layer of saltine crackers in the pan. If needed, cut crackers in half to fill the last strip in the pan.
4. In a saucepan, melt the butter on medium heat. Remove from heat and stir in the brown sugar.
5. Return to the heat. Bring the mixture to a boil, reduce the heat to low, and cook for 2½ minutes, stirring often.
6. Pour the buttery syrup over the crackers. Spread the syrup evenly with a rubber spatula. Bake 5 minutes.
7. Carefully remove the baking pan and place it on a cooling rack.
8. Sprinkle the chocolate chips on top. Return the pan to the oven for 1 minute to melt the chocolate.
9. Remove the pan from the oven, place it on a cooling rack, and spread the chocolate chips with a metal spatula or table knife to make an even layer of chocolate.
10. Sprinkle the almonds on top and pat them down with a spoon or spatula. Cool until the candy is hardened. (It will cool faster if refrigerated.)

Notes:

11. When the candy is cool and hardened, cut or break it into pieces. Store the candy in a covered container in a cool place.

Makes about 48 pieces

Note: If you don't have a jelly roll pan, use a 9 x 13-inch pan and an 8 x 8-inch pan. Pour ⅔ of the syrup over the crackers in the larger pan and ⅓ of the syrup over the crackers in the square pan.

Variations:

- Replace the dark chocolate chips with semisweet chocolate chips.
- Substitute walnuts, pecans, or nuts of your choice for the almonds. Or replace the nuts with white chocolate chips and dried cranberries.
- Replace the saltine crackers with graham crackers.

Year-Round

Blowing out birthday candles, traveling to family events, and seeing new sights. Look for reasons and seasons to celebrate all year. Make memories in the kitchen stirring up tasty foods from this cookbook. Or pull out favorite recipes from your heritage and introduce them to your grandkids. As you share time together, your family relationships will grow.

There is a time for everything, and a season for every activity under the heavens.

ECCLESIASTES 3:1

Year-Round

Notes:

Meat Turnovers

Shiberecky—a favorite childhood food of mine—has become one of my grandchildren's favorites too. I included it at my granddaughters' request and modified the recipe to make it easier to prepare. We think you're in for a treat if you make them. (*Recipe from the kitchen of my mother, Helena Siemens.*)

Difficulty:

Prep time: 30 minutes
Baking time: 15 minutes

Gather with Grandma

1 T. oil
½ pound lean ground beef
2 T. fresh onion, minced
Scant ½ tsp. salt
⅛ tsp. pepper, or to taste
⅓ to ½ cup hot water
2 tubes prepared biscuits (8 to 10 biscuits per tube)
Butter-flavored nonstick cooking spray
Ketchup (optional)

Make with Grandma

1. Preheat the oven to 375°. Prepare a 9 x 13-inch baking pan or larger pan with sides by spreading 1 tablespoon oil in the bottom of the pan.
2. In a medium-sized bowl, combine the meat, onion, and seasonings.
3. Stir in ⅓ cup water. Add additional water, a tablespoon at a time up to ½ cup total, until the meat mixture is moist but not runny. The water will make the meat juicy and tender as it bakes.
4. On a lightly floured surface, roll out 1 biscuit at a time into a 3-inch circle.
5. Put a tablespoon of the meat mixture in the center of the biscuit and fold it over to make a half-circle turnover. Seal the edges well by pinching them together.
6. Place the turnovers in the baking pan and spray the top of each one with butter spray. Bake the turnovers about 10 to 12 minutes. Check the turnovers after 8 minutes to see if they are browning on the top. If not, carefully

Notes:

remove the pan with meat turnovers from the oven, turn them over, and continue baking them.

7. When browned, remove the turnovers from the oven. Cut 1 turnover in half to make sure the meat is no longer pink. They should be done, but if not, bake them a short time longer.
8. If desired, serve them with ketchup. Refrigerate or freeze the leftovers.

Makes 16 to 20 meat turnovers

Notes:

Personal Pizzas with Pizzazz

What grandkid doesn't love pizza? They're perfect for a party or any meal. Organize a pizza bar with toppings and let each person create his or her own pizza. Grand-sized biscuits and ready-made sauce make these pizzas quick to make and bake.

Difficulty:

Prep time: 20 minutes
Baking time: 10 to 12 minutes

Gather with Grandma

1 (16 oz.) tube of grand biscuits (jumbo size)
Flour to dust the work surface
1 (14 oz.) jar pizza sauce
Toppings for pizza bar, such as:
- Black olives, sliced
- Any color pepper, chopped (green, orange, red, or yellow)
- Mushrooms, sliced
- Tomatoes, sliced
- Onion, thinly sliced
- Pineapple tidbits, drained
- Canadian bacon slices
- Bacon, cooked and crumbled
- Ground beef, browned
- Pepperoni, sliced thin
- Sausage, cooked and crumbled
- Mozzarella cheese, grated
- Italian seasoning

Make with Grandma

1. Preheat the oven to 375°. Prepare pizza pans, baking sheets, or individual cake pans with nonstick cooking spray.
2. Lightly flour a work surface. Roll out jumbo biscuits to 4½ or 5 inches. Place them on the baking sheet.
3. Spoon 1 heaping tablespoon pizza sauce on each to cover the dough, leaving a ½-inch circle of dough without sauce.

Notes:

4. Add the toppings you like to each mini pizza.
5. Top with cheese. Sprinkle with Italian seasoning to add pizzazz.
6. Bake for 10 to 12 minutes until the crust is brown and the cheese is melted.
7. Carefully remove the pizzas from the oven. Place pizzas on a cooling rack for a few minutes. Because the pizzas are personal size, you get to eat a whole pizza by yourself, and maybe even more than one! Enjoy with your favorite beverage.

Makes 8 individual pizzas

Variation: Make Pizza Puffs with Pizzazz. Spray muffin cups with nonstick cooking spray. Cut the grand-size biscuits in half. (Or use whole biscuits from a tube of regular-size biscuits.) Flatten them and place one-half biscuit in each cup. Add sauce, toppings, cheese, and Italian seasoning. Bake at 375° for 8 to 10 minutes, or until the crust is brown and the cheese is melted. Yummy and cute!

A Spoonful of Sharing

When I asked my grandkids what they usually eat at birthday parties, they said, "Pizza!" As you eat your pizzas, describe one of the best birthdays you have ever celebrated. What made it great?

Notes:

Candle Salad

Fun to make for birthdays, Christmas, or to enjoy anytime.

Difficulty:

Prep time: 15 minutes
Gluten-free

Gather with Grandma

4 large lettuce leaves
1 (8 oz.) can pineapple rings (4 rings)
2 bananas (as straight as possible)
Toothpicks
4 maraschino cherry "flames" (or mandarin orange slices or pieces of orange gumdrops)

Make with Grandma

1. Wash the lettuce leaves, pat them dry, and place 1 leaf on each plate.
2. Drain the pineapple and then place 1 pineapple ring on each leaf.
3. Peel the bananas. Cut each banana in half across the middle to make 2 candles from each one. Cut the curved ends off each banana.
4. Place the thickest part of the banana halves in the center of the rings.
5. Use a toothpick to attach a cherry "flame" on the top of each banana candle.

Makes 4 candle salads

A Spoonful of Sharing

Names have meanings, and my granddaughter Clara's name means "bright." She *is* smart, but bright here means light. Her mom framed Matthew 5:16 for her room. It says: Clara: Bright. "Let your light shine before men, that they may see your good deeds and praise your Father in heaven."

Jesus is the Light of the world (John 8:12), and He helps us shine bright for Him. How can we be lights to others?

Notes:

Crisp Veggie Scepters

Rule with your scepters and then eat them!

Difficulty:

Prep time: 15 minutes
Gluten-free

Gather with Grandma

1 long celery stalk
1 long, thin carrot
1 large pitted black olive
¼ cup ranch dressing

Make with Grandma

Celery Scepters

1. Wash the celery stalk. Trim the ends.
2. Slit the narrow end of the stalk with several vertical cuts about 1 inch long.
3. Place the celery into a bowl of ice water and refrigerate it for at least 30 minutes or until the slit end opens.
4. Now you have a celery scepter!

Carrot Scepters

1. Wash the carrot and peel it with a vegetable peeler.
2. Place a pitted black olive on the pointed end.
3. After you finish reigning with your scepters, dip them into salad dressing and munch on them!

See the recipe for Ranch Dressing and Dip on page 148.

Make as many as you need

Notes:

Fresh Veggie Cups

Almost as fresh tasting as picking veggies right from the garden. This recipe makes an appealing way to serve veggies indoors or outdoors at a picnic.

Difficulty:

Prep time: 15 minutes
Gluten-free

Gather with Grandma

- Clear plastic dessert cups or short glasses
- Favorite salad dressing or dip
- Colorful, fresh vegetables. Select your favorites, such as:
  - Green: cucumber sticks, asparagus spears, pea pods, zucchini sticks, green beans, celery sticks
  - Orange: carrot sticks, orange pepper strips
  - Red: red pepper strips, cherry or grape tomatoes, radishes
  - Yellow: yellow pepper strips, crookneck squash or yellow zucchini sticks
- Toothpicks

Make with Grandma

1. Spoon a tablespoon of your favorite salad dressing or dip into the bottom of a clear plastic cup.
2. Place an assortment of colorful fresh vegetables in the cup using at least 3 colors. Place shorter veggies, such as tomatoes and radishes, on picks.
3. Prepare 1 cup for each person. Or set out a tray of assorted veggies and let individuals fill their own cups with dip and favorite veggies.
4. Dip the vegetables into the dressing as you eat them.

Make as many as you need

Tip: To make the ends of celery sticks curl, make 3 or 4 half-inch cuts at 1 or both ends of the celery. Place the celery in a bowl of ice water and refrigerate it. The ends of the celery will start to curl in about 30 minutes.

Notes:

Ranch Dressing and Dip

My grandkids like to dip fresh veggies into ranch dressing. This recipe passed their taste test with a thumbs-up. It also tastes delicious as a sandwich spread and on vegetable salads.

Difficulty: 

Prep time: 10 minutes
Chill time: 1 hour
Gluten-free

Gather with Grandma

1 cup mayonnaise
½ cup sour cream
2 tsp. minced dried onion
1 tsp. dried parsley flakes
¼ tsp. garlic powder
⅛ tsp. salt or to taste
Dash of pepper to taste
½ tsp. dried dill (optional)
1 tsp. fresh lemon juice (optional)

Make with Grandma

1. Combine the mayonnaise and sour cream in a medium-sized bowl.
2. In a small dish, mix the seasonings together with a fork.
3. Add the seasonings and lemon juice (if desired) to the mayonnaise mixture and stir with a wire whip until blended.
4. Spoon the mixture into a small jar and cover it with a lid. Chill the dressing for an hour or more to blend the flavors.
5. Keep the dressing refrigerated. It stays fresh for 3 weeks.

Makes 1½ cups dressing

Tip: For a thinner salad dressing, add milk, 1 tablespoon at a time, until you have the desired consistency.

Notes:

Chocolate Crispy Crunchies

This yummy, crunchy, and easy-to-make mix is a great party snack or gift. My granddaughters request this favorite snack as Christmas and birthday gifts.

Difficulty: 

Prep time: 20 minutes
Chill time: 20 minutes

Gather with Grandma

4 cups Chex cereal (rice, corn, wheat, chocolate, or a mixture)
½ cup semisweet chocolate chips
¼ cup creamy peanut butter
2 T. butter
½ tsp. vanilla
1 cup powdered sugar, divided

Make with Grandma

1. Measure the cereal into a large bowl. Set it aside.
2. In a microwave-safe bowl, combine the chocolate chips, peanut butter, and butter. Microwave on high for 30 seconds and stir. Continue to microwave and stir the mixture at 30-second intervals until it is melted and smooth.
3. Stir in the vanilla.
4. Pour the chocolate mixture over the cereal. Stir until the cereal is evenly coated. It will be lightly covered.
5. Pour ¾ cup powdered sugar into a gallon-sized resealable bag. Add the cereal and shake the bag until the mixture is well coated.
6. Place the bag of Chocolate Crispy Crunchies in the refrigerator for 20 minutes or until the chocolate mixture hardens.
7. Add ¼ cup powdered sugar to the bag and shake it to further coat the mix. Store the snack in the refrigerator in the sealed plastic bag or in an airtight container. You probably won't need to store it for long!

Makes 4 cups

Variation: Use other chip flavors, such as butterscotch.

Notes:

Golden Tortilla Crowns

Just right for regal princes and princesses. (*Created by Grandma Tea and Owen when he was four years old.*)

Difficulty:

Prep time: 10 minutes

Gather with Grandma

2 6-inch flour tortillas
½ cup cheddar cheese, finely grated
Sliced green and/or black olives for jewels
Carrot circles or diced red and green peppers for jewels

Make with Grandma

1. Cut tortillas in half with a pizza cutter or table knife.
2. The straight edge is the bottom of the crown. Starting in the middle of the rounded edge, cut out 2 V-shaped notches—1 on each side—to make the points of a crown. Repeat for each tortilla half.
3. Place crowns on a microwave-safe plate. Top each crown with grated cheese.
4. Add olive and/or vegetable jewels, if desired.
5. Microwave the crowns for 30 seconds or until the cheese melts. Be careful. The tortillas will be hot and soft.
6. Eat them with your best regal manners.

Makes 4 crowns

Variation: For cinnamon-and-sugar crowns, sprinkle them with a mixture of 1 tablespoon sugar and 1 teaspoon cinnamon. Warm them in the microwave.

Notes:

A Spoonful of Sharing

Every year we celebrate our grandchildren's spiritual birthdays with a party. One year we used a royal theme, and the grandkids wore crowns with "King Jesus" on them. These parties are a wonderful time to talk about Jesus and the gift of eternal life. For more information about joining God's family, see "Sharing Your Faith with Your Grandchildren" on page 169. Sharing the gospel with ten words and using hand motions is a simple way to tell children and adults about Jesus.

Notes:

Berry Good Freezer Jam

This low-sugar, uncooked jam tastes like fresh fruit. When berries are in season, my youngest grandson, Owen, and I make several batches of blackberry and raspberry jam together. Proud of his tasty product, he labels the containers "Owen's Jam." We sample it on toast, and he takes jam home to share. This fun and easy jam makes a delicious shared experience for us.

Difficulty:

Prep time: 20 to 25 minutes
Gluten-free

Gather with Grandma

5 cups fresh raspberries, washed
1 cup sugar
3 T. instant pectin (comes in a jar)

Make with Grandma

1. Pour 1 cup berries into a flat pan with sides and mash them. Or put the berries into a sealed plastic bag to crush them. Spoon the berries into a measuring cup. The crushed berries will measure less than a cup.
2. Repeat mashing the berries, 1 cup at a time, until you have 2½ cups crushed fruit. (You may have some whole berries left.)
3. Mix the sugar and instant pectin together in a large bowl. Add the crushed fruit and stir the mixture with a wooden spoon for 3 minutes.
4. Ladle the jam into clean 8-ounce jars or plastic containers, leaving ½-inch space at the top because the jam will expand as it freezes. (This recipe should fill 3 jars with a little extra to sample.) Let the jam sit for 30 minutes. Then refrigerate 1 container to eat and freeze the others.
5. Serve the jam on scones, biscuits, toast, or ice cream.
6. The jam can be stored up to 3 weeks in the refrigerator and for a year in the freezer.

Makes about 3½ cups freezer jam

Variations: Blackberry or Strawberry Jam: For blackberries, follow the recipe

Notes:

using fresh or frozen, thawed blackberries. For strawberries, hull the berries and slice them. Crush enough berries to make 2½ cups of fruit.

Tip: Less seeds: After you crush the berries, strain some of the seeds out through a strainer. I do this with the raspberry jam and sometimes with the blackberry jam.

A Spoonful of Sharing

While my son and his wife were away for their anniversary, both sets of grandparents had the joy of watching the grandkids. When it was time to return the "joybringers," both grandparents' cars arrived at the same time. Clara jumped out of their car and ran toward us. "It's a party!" she said. "Both sets of grandparents are here!" Her spontaneous excitement thrilled me. Families are an important part of God's plan. Psalm 68:6 (NLT) says, "God places the lonely in families." What makes your family special?

Notes:

Ice Cream Bread

Here's the scoop: Combining ice cream and flour gives you cake and ice cream in one bite! Make it with your favorite flavor of ice cream. Strawberry or chocolate chip mint bread makes a tasty treat or gift.

Difficulty:

Prep time: 10 minutes
Baking time: 25 to 30 minutes

Gather with Grandma

1 cup ice cream, softened
¾ cup self-rising flour
1 T. sugar (optional)

Make with Grandma

1. Preheat the oven to 350°. Spray a small loaf pan with nonstick cooking spray.
2. Measure the ice cream into a medium-sized bowl and stir until smooth.
3. Add flour and sugar if desired. Stir until blended.
4. Spoon the batter into the loaf pan.
5. Bake for 25 to 30 minutes or until a toothpick poked into the center comes out clean.
6. Cool for 10 minutes on a cooling rack. Loosen the sides with a knife and remove the bread from the baking pan.
7. When cool, slice the bread and serve it by itself or with a scoop of the same flavor ice cream. Wrap and refrigerate leftovers.

Tip: To make self-rising flour, whisk together ¾ cup flour, 1 tsp. baking powder, and ¼ tsp. salt. Store the flour mixture in a covered container.

Notes:

Rolling Pancakes

This favorite of my grandkids comes from the kitchen of my sister, MaryAnn. They are really crepes, but her son called them rolling pancakes because you roll them up. My granddaughter Anna likes them topped with strawberries, whipped cream, and pink and purple sprinkles.

Difficulty:

Prep time: 15 minutes
Cooking time: 20 minutes

Gather with Grandma

4 eggs
1 cup flour
1 T. sugar
1⅓ cups milk
1 tsp. vanilla
¼ cup (½ stick) butter for frying
Toppings of choice: powdered sugar, jam, syrup, honey, whipped cream, and/or fruit

Make with Grandma

1. In a medium-sized bowl, beat the eggs.
2. Add the flour, sugar, milk, and vanilla. Mix well.
3. Preheat a griddle or frying pan to medium heat.
4. Add 1 teaspoon butter. When melted, pour in ¼ cup pancake batter and spread it into a circle by tilting the pan.
5. Cook until light brown on one side. Turn and brown on the other side.
6. Remove the pancake to a plate. When cool enough to handle, roll it up.
7. Continue with the rest of the batter. Melt butter in the pan for each pancake.
8. I serve them rolled up. Then the grandkids unroll them to add fillings and toppings they like.

See page 152 for Berry Good Freezer Jam and page 38 for Homemade Whipped Cream.

Makes 12 6-inch pancakes

Notes:

Cascade Blackberry Pie

This is our grandson Alex's favorite pie. You might say blackberry pie is his love language. Alex's Grandma Cheryl grows the berries in her yard and shares them with us. This pie tastes so yummy that we allow licking the plate to get the last bit of juicy flavor.

Difficulty: 3 spoons

Prep time: 30 minutes
Baking time: 45 minutes
Gluten-free option: Use tapioca to thicken the berries and a premade gluten-free crust

Gather with Grandma

Fruit Filling

1 cup sugar
3 T. tapioca (or flour)
3½ cups blackberries (thaw if frozen)
1 T. butter (to dot on fruit filling)

Piecrust

2 cups flour
¾ tsp. salt
¾ cup plus 2 T. shortening
1 egg, beaten
3 to 4 T. cold water
1 tsp. granulated sugar to sprinkle on top
Ice cream (optional)

Make with Grandma

1. Preheat the oven to 425°.
2. For the fruit filling, combine the sugar and tapioca or flour in a large bowl. Mix in the berries. Set the filling aside.
3. For the crust, mix the flour and salt together in another large bowl. Cut in the shortening until the particles are the size of peas.
4. Mix together the egg and 3 tablespoons water. Add them to the flour and shortening mixture and mix the dough with a fork. If the dough is dry, add 1 more tablespoon water.

Notes:

5. Gather the dough into a ball and divide it in half to make 2 crusts.
6. Roll half the dough on a pastry cloth or floured surface into a 10-inch circle about ⅛-inch thick.
7. Place the bottom crust in the 9-inch pie pan. Add the fruit mixture and dot it with butter.
8. Roll out the top crust in the same way and place it on top of the fruit.
9. Using a table knife, cut off the extra dough around the edge of the pie pan. Seal the edges and form a fluted edge.
10. Cut a few slits in the top crust and sprinkle it with sugar if desired. I make slits in the shape of a large *A* when I make it for Alex.
11. Place the pie on a cookie sheet to catch any juice that may bubble over while it bakes.
12. Bake the pie for 15 minutes at 425°. Then reduce the temperature to 375° and bake the pie for 25 to 30 additional minutes or until the crust is golden brown and the filling bubbles. Place the pie on a cooling rack for several hours to cool and thicken.
13. Serve with ice cream if desired.

Makes 6 to 8 servings

Tip: If you don't have Cascade blackberries, substitute marionberries, boysenberries, blueberries, or mixed berries.

Notes:

Everyone's Favorite Cookies

I discovered the recipe for *Brun Kaker*—a crisp, buttery, Scandinavian cookie—in our church cookbook decades ago. The recipe quickly became a family favorite, and I've yet to find anyone who doesn't like them. For special holidays, add a few colorful sprinkles before baking. The key ingredient is golden syrup. (*From the kitchen of Grandma Julie.*)

Difficulty:

Prep time: 15 minutes
Baking time: 15 to 20 minutes for each baking sheet of cookies

Gather with Grandma

1 cup (2 sticks) butter, softened
1 cup granulated sugar
2 T. powdered sugar
2 T. golden syrup (e.g., Lyle's)
1 tsp. vanilla
2 cups flour
1 tsp. baking soda

Make with Grandma

1. Preheat the oven to 350°.
2. In a large bowl, cream together the butter, sugars, golden syrup, and vanilla.
3. In a medium-sized bowl, mix together the flour and baking soda.
4. Add the dry ingredients to the creamed mixture, 1 cup at a time. Mix until blended. You may want to mix it by hand.
5. Divide the dough in half. Form each part into 2 long rolls, about 1½ inches in diameter.
6. Place 2 rolls of dough on an ungreased baking sheet. Bake the cookies for 15 to 20 minutes, or until the rolls have flattened and are lightly browned.
7. Remove the cookies from the oven and place the cookie sheet on a cooling rack. Using a pizza cutter or knife, cut each rope into diagonal strips that are 1 inch wide. Allow the cookies to cool slightly before moving them from the pan to cooling racks. When cool, store the cookies in a covered container.

Makes 3 to 4 dozen cookies

Tip: You can find golden syrup in some grocery stores shelved near light and dark corn syrup, and also online. Although you could replace golden syrup with dark corn syrup, the cookies will not have the same distinctive flavor that makes them delicious and popular.

A Spoonful of Sharing

What are some of your favorite foods and recipes? How did they become family favorites?

Notes:

Notes:

Grandma's Yum-Delicious Baked Custard

Healthy and easy to make. A favorite of my grandchildren. I started making this for our first young grandchild, Peter, because it was soft and nutritious. It's still a favorite at family dinners. I bake it in individual ramekins.

Difficulty:

Prep time: 10 minutes
Bake time: 35 to 45 minutes
Gluten-free

Gather with Grandma

2 cups milk
2 large eggs, beaten
⅓ cup sugar
1 tsp. vanilla
¼ tsp. salt
Nutmeg to sprinkle on top

Make with Grandma

1. Preheat the oven to 350°.
2. Heat the milk to about 120°.
3. In a medium-sized bowl, whisk together the eggs, sugar, vanilla, and salt.
4. Gradually stir in the milk and mix well.
5. Pour the custard into a 1½-quart baking dish or 5 or 6 custard cups.
6. Set the custard dish(es) in a baking pan and fill the pan with 1 inch of water to create a water bath.
7. Lightly sprinkle nutmeg on top of the custard.
8. Bake the custard for 45 minutes if made in a baking dish. If made in custard cups, test for doneness after 35 minutes. The custard is done when a knife inserted 1 inch from the edge comes out clean. When done, remove the custard and let it cool.
9. Serve warm or chilled. Refrigerate leftovers.

Makes 6 servings

Notes:

Honey-Bun Cake

This favorite cake of Grandma Dianna's grandchildren melts in your mouth. Her grandchildren often request it for their birthdays. My grandkids like it too.

Difficulty:

Prep time: 20 minutes
Baking time: 40 to 45 minutes

Gather with Grandma

Cake

1 (15.25 oz.) box yellow cake mix
4 eggs
1 cup sour cream
¾ cup vegetable oil
½ cup light brown sugar
2 tsp. cinnamon

Glaze

1½ cups powdered sugar
3 T. milk
½ tsp. vanilla flavoring or extract

Make with Grandma

1. Preheat the oven to 325°. Spray a 9 x 13-inch pan with nonstick cooking spray.
2. In a large bowl, mix together all of the cake ingredients until well blended (about 2 minutes).
3. Pour the cake batter into the prepared pan, spreading the batter evenly.
4. Bake the cake for 40 minutes or until a toothpick inserted in the center comes out clean.
5. While the cake is baking, make the glaze. Mix the powdered sugar, milk, and vanilla together until the glaze is the desired consistency
6. After baking, place the pan with the cake on a cooling rack. Pour the glaze on the warm cake. Tilt the pan to spread the glaze evenly or spread it with a rubber spatula.
7. Serve the cake with fresh strawberries and ice cream if desired.

Makes 15 servings

Notes:

No-Bake Chocolate Éclair Cake

You'll be surprised that these ingredients turn into a delicious cake after several hours in the refrigerator. Nana Bay says, "My son just turned fifty, and he has requested this cake for his birthday since he was ten! Now my grandkids love it."

Difficulty:

Prep Time: 20 minutes
Chilling time: 8 hours

Gather with Grandma

1 tsp. butter
1 (14.4 oz) box graham crackers (you'll have some left)
1 (5.1 oz.) vanilla instant pudding
3 cups cold milk
1 (8 oz.) container frozen whipped topping, slightly thawed (e.g., Cool Whip)
1 (16 oz.) can ready-made chocolate frosting
Fresh strawberries or raspberries, washed

Make with Grandma

1. Butter a 9 x 13-inch cake pan. Cover the bottom of the pan with whole (two squares together) graham crackers (not crushed). Fill in any smaller remaining space with partial crackers.
2. In a large bowl, whisk together the pudding mix and the milk until blended.
3. Mix in the whipped topping.
4. Spoon half the pudding over the graham crackers and smooth the filling with a rubber spatula to make an even layer.
5. Place another layer of whole graham crackers on top of the pudding.
6. Spoon the rest of the pudding mixture over the crackers and smooth it into an even layer.
7. Top the pudding with another layer of graham crackers.
8. Spoon the frosting on top. Carefully spread the frosting over the top layer of the crackers. Use all the frosting (or less if you prefer a thinner layer).
9. Cover and refrigerate the cake for 8 hours or longer.

Notes:

10. To serve the cake, cut it into 12 pieces and garnish each piece with a fresh strawberry or a few raspberries. Refrigerate the leftovers in a covered container.

Serves 12

Variation: Replace the large package of vanilla pudding with 1 small package instant vanilla pudding and 1 small package instant chocolate pudding. Mix each pudding in a separate bowl according to the package directions. Fold 1 cup topping into each pudding. Layer the pudding this way: a layer of graham crackers on the bottom, chocolate pudding, graham crackers, vanilla pudding, graham crackers, and chocolate frosting. Cover and chill for 8 hours or longer.

Tip: If you use this for a birthday cake, place fresh raspberries upside down on top of the cake and use them as candleholders. Place a birthday candle in each raspberry, or as needed for the age of the person.

A Spoonful of Sharing

Kids love birthday parties with cake, candles, ice cream, and presents. Did you know there are parties in heaven for another kind of birth? The angels celebrate each time someone on earth chooses to follow God and become part of His family. "There is joy in the presence of God's angels when even one sinner repents" (Luke 15:10 NLT). You can read more about this in Luke 15:1-10.

Holidays and Special Days with Menu Suggestions

Happy New Year:
Sleepover Pajama Party
Sausage Triangles
Banana Split Bowls
Funtastic New Year's Pretzels
Midnight Munchies
Puffy Pancake (for breakfast)

Winter Fun: *Snowy Day Delights*
Tasty Toboggans
Edible Igloos
Floating Frosty Snowmen
Snowman's Delight Hot Chocolate

Valentine's Day: *Sharing Love, Smiles, and Goodies*
Smiley Joes
Fresh Strawberry Hearts and Dip
Great Grins
Double-Thumbprint Heart Cookies
Soda Cracker Toffee

St. Patrick's Day: *Green Cuisine*
Crock-Pot Irish Stew
7UP Shamrock Biscuits
Irish Fresh Fruit Flag
Shamrock Sundaes

Easter: *Sunrise Surprises*
Easter Egg-Stravaganza
Ham and Swiss Cheese Melts
Peter Rabbit's Carrot Patch and Hummus
Sparkling Sonrise Fruit Parfaits
Hot Cross Buns

Cinco de Mayo: *Taste of Mexico*
Sombrero Skillet Pie
Mexican Veggie Flag
Cinnamon Chips
Fiesta Fruit Salsa
Apple Enchiladas

Mother's Day: *Brunch for a Peach of a Mom*
Sealed with a Quiche
Sweet or Savory Bacon Knots
Hugs and Kisses for Mom
Fancy Fruit Bouquets
Peaches and Cream Cobbler

Spring Fun: *Cute Critters to Make and Munch*
Butterfly Waffles
Bananapillars
Ladybug Cheese and Crackers
Apple Posies and Buzzy Bee Snacks

Father's Day: *Home Run Hits for Dad*
Grand-Slam Pulled Pork Sandwiches
Out-of-the-Park Cheesy Potatoes
Triple Play Bean Salad
Batter Balls
Root Beer Float Cookie Sandwiches

Fourth of July: *Patriotic Picnic*
Freedom Franks in Blankets
Zippy Dip
Frosty Fruit Sparklers
Patriotic Punch
Show Your Colors Cupcakes

Celebrate Friendship: *Tea for Two*
Chicken Salad Sandwiches
Scone Blossoms
Luscious Lemon Curd
Berry Good Freezer Jam
Chilled Strawberry Soup
Triple Treat Triangles

Summer Fun: *Seashore Snacks*
Clamshell Tuna Sandwiches
Seashell Pasta Salad
Honeydew Canoes
Goin' Fishin' Snack Mix
Sandbar Surprises

Grandparents Day: *Teddy Bear Picnic*
Build-Your-Bear Sandwiches
Mac 'n' Cheese Cups
Veggie Wagons
Handmade Fruit Pie
Teddy Bear Munch Mix

Taste of Space: *Out-of-this-World Treats*
Blast Off Rocket Snack
Telescope Roll-Ups
Meat-eor Bites
Solar Eclipse Toast

Fall Fun: *Pumpkin-Patch Party*
A-Maze-ing Corn Chowder with Sausage
Easy Batter Bread
Candy Corn Popcorn Cake
Pumpkin Patch Cheese Balls
Acorn Treats

Thanksgiving: *Harvest Your Blessings*
Fruity Turkey Favors
Frosty Cranberry Circles
Cornbread Pilgrim Hats
Frost on the Pumpkin Dessert
Sugar 'n' Spice Pecans

Christmas: *Cool Yule Yummies*
Savory Holiday Meatballs
Crisp Veggie Wreath and Dip
Peppermint Angel Cake
Cranberry Shortcake with Butter-Rum Sauce
Frosted Nativity Cookies

Happy Birthday to You! Light the Candles
Personal Pizzas with Pizzazz
Candle Salad
Fresh Veggie Cups and Ranch Dressing and Dip
Honey-Bun Cake
Chocolate Crispy Crunchies

Spiritual Birthdays: *Royal Recipes for Kingdom Kids*

Golden Tortilla Crowns

Crisp Veggie Scepters

No-Bake Chocolate Éclair Cake

Ice Cream Bread

Celebrate Family: *Sharing Favorite Recipes*

Meat Turnovers

Grandma's Yum-Delicious Baked Custard

Rolling Pancakes

Cascade Blackberry Pie

Everyone's Favorite Cookies

Sharing Your Faith with Your Grandchildren

These verses will help you share the gospel with your grandchildren. In just five steps, you can explain how to invite Jesus into their life and ask Him to guide them. You can read this to your grandchild or put it in your own words.

1. God loves.

"God so loved the world that he gave his one and only Son, that whoever believes in him shall not perish but have eternal life" (John 3:16).

God loves you and always will. He wants you to accept Jesus as your personal Savior and live with Him forever.

2. We sinned.

"All have sinned and fall short of the glory of God" (Romans 3:23).

Because of our sins (anything we do or think that is wrong), we are separated from God, who is holy and sinless. We all need God's forgiveness.

3. Jesus died.

"God demonstrates his own love for us in this: While we were still sinners, Christ died for us" (Romans 5:8).

God had a plan to bring us back to Him. He sent His Son Jesus to die on the cross to save us from our sins.

4. God forgives.

"If we confess our sins, he is faithful and just and will forgive us our sins and purify us from all unrighteousness" (1 John 1:9).

If we admit that we do wrong and ask God to forgive us, He will.

5. We accept.

"To all who did receive him, to those who believed in his name, he gave the right to become children of God" (John 1:12).

Once we accept God's free gift of salvation, which comes through Jesus, we become God's children.

How to Share the Gospel in Ten Words with Hand Motions

You can also share the ten-word salvation message with hand motions. Start by holding up both hands. The right hand represents God, and the left hand represents people. Repeat the words in bold aloud as you do the motions.

1. (Both hands are clasped together.)

   "God loves."

2. (Left hand moves to the left.)

   "We sinned."

3. (Right hand moves to the right.)

   "Jesus died."

4. (Now both hands are stretched out to form a cross. Then the right hand moves to center.)

   "God forgives."

5. (Left hand moves to center and clasps the right hand.)

   "We accept."

If your grandchild wants to turn his or her life over to God, pray together using a prayer something like this:

> Dear God, I know I'm a sinner. Thank You for sending Jesus to die for my sins and rise from the dead. Please forgive my sins. I want to stop doing wrong things and receive

Jesus as my Lord and Savior. Thank You for forgiving me and making me Your child. I want to obey and follow You. In Jesus's name. Amen.

If your grandchild prayed this prayer in faith, then 2 Corinthians 5:17 is true of him or her: *"If anyone is in Christ, the new creation has come: The old has gone, the new is here!"*

To help your grandchild grow in Christ:

1. Encourage your grandchild to tell someone about his or her new faith in Christ.
2. If possible, help your grandchild find and attend a church that solidly teaches the Bible.
3. Teach your grandchild to pray every day and read the Bible—God's love letter to each of us.
4. Consider giving your grandchild an age-appropriate Bible and devotional book to help him or her grow in faith.

You can receive a free weekly devotional at billygraham.org/decision. If you have questions or need help to grow spiritually, e-mail: help@bgea.org.

(Adapted from *Preparing My Heart for Grandparenting: For Grandparents at Any Stage of the Journey*, Lydia E. Harris, AMG Publishers, 2010.)

Index

Salads and Sides

Snacks

About the Author

Lydia E. Harris loves to develop and test recipes with her grandchildren. Her recipes have appeared in two children's cookbooks and several magazines, including *Pockets* and Focus on the Family's *Clubhouse Jr.*, *Clubhouse*, and *Brio.*

Her bimonthly column, "A Cup of Tea with Lydia," has been published in *The Country Register* in the US and Canada for almost two decades and reaches approximately 500,000 readers.

Lydia has also contributed to numerous books and is the author of *Preparing My Heart for Grandparenting: For Grandparents at Any Stage of the Journey.*

She earned her master's degree in Home Economics at the University of Washington, where she met her husband, Milt. They have been married for more than 50 years and enjoy spending time with their two married children and five grandchildren.